BATTLE OF LEYTE GULF

THE LARGEST SEA BATTLE OF THE SECOND WORLD WAR

BATTLE OF LEYTE GULF

THE LARGEST SEA BATTLE OF THE SECOND WORLD WAR

John Grehan and Alexander Nicoll

Frontline Books

BATTLE OF LEYTE GULF
The Largest Sea Battle of the Second World War

First published in Great Britain in 2021 by Frontline Books,
an imprint of Pen & Sword Books Ltd,
Yorkshire – Philadelphia

Copyright © John Grehan and Alexander Nicoll
ISBN: 978-1-52677-039-4

The right of © John Grehan and Alexander Nicoll to be identified as Authors of this work has been asserted by them in accordance with the Copyright, Designs and Patents Act 1988. A CIP catalogue record for this book is available from the British Library All rights reserved.

No part of this book may be reproduced or transmitted in any form or by any means, electronic or mechanical including photocopying, recording or by any information storage and retrieval system, without permission from the Publisher in writing.

Typeset in Avenir 9.5/12.5 by Dave Cassan

Pen & Sword Books Ltd incorporates the imprints of Air World Books, Pen & Sword Archaeology, Atlas, Aviation, Battleground, Discovery, Family History, History, Maritime, Military, Naval, Politics, Social History, Transport, True Crime, Claymore Press, Frontline Books, Praetorian Press, Seaforth Publishing and White Owl.

For a complete list of Pen & Sword titles please contact:

PEN & SWORD BOOKS LTD
47 Church Street, Barnsley, South Yorkshire, S70 2AS, UK.
E-mail: enquiries@pen-and-sword.co.uk
Website: www.pen-and-sword.co.uk

or

PEN AND SWORD BOOKS,
1950 Lawrence Road, Havertown, PA 19083, USA
E-mail: Uspen-and-sword@casematepublishers.com
Website: www.penandswordbooks.com

Printed and bound by CPI Group (UK) Ltd, Croydon, CR0 4YY

CONTENTS

Acknowledgements		vi
Introduction – The Invasion of the Philippines		vii
Chapter 1	The Leyte Landings	1
Chapter 2	The Japanese Naval Forces	35
Chapter 3	Battle of the Sibuyan Sea: 24 October 1944	41
Chapter 4	Battles of the Sulu Sea and the Surigao Strait: 24-25 October 1944	76
Chapter 5	The Battle off Samar: 25 October 1944	95
Chapter 6	Battle off Cape Engaño: 25-26 October 1944	145
Chapter 7	Consequences and Controversies	175
References and Notes		184

ACKNOWLEDGEMENTS

The authors and publisher would like to extend their grateful thanks, in no particular order, to the following individuals and organisations for their assistance with the images used in this publication: Robert Mitchell, James Luto, Historic Military Press, US Naval History and Heritage Command, US National Museum of Naval Aviation, US National Archives and Records Administration, National Museum of the US Air Force, United States Air Force, US Navy, and the US Library of Congress.

INTRODUCTION
The Invasion of The Philippines

The great wave of Japanese aggression which in nine months carried the Emperor's forces halfway across the Pacific, began to recede with the loss of Guadalcanal in the first weeks of 1943. During the fourteen months since Pearl Harbor, the Allies, primarily the Americans, had laid a solid foundation for the recovery of their lost territories. Across the Pacific, from the American continent to Australia and New Zealand, a long chain of island bases had been established, to guard the communications, permit the servicing of naval ships and aircraft, and facilitate the transport of great hosts of men and vast quantities of equipment and stores needed for the extensive and arduous operations to come.

The factories and shipyards of the Allied nations had also been furiously at work. In the autumn of 1942, the US had just three aircraft carriers in the Pacific. By the end of 1943, there were no less than fifty American carriers operating in the Pacific. That massive output enabled the Allies to mount an offensive operation that would eventually take them to the outlying islands of Japan itself.

That offensive took the form of a dual advance across the Pacific. From the south, General of the Army Douglas MacArthur led a combined Army and Navy force which fought its way northwards from Australia and New Caledonia along the north coast of New Guinea to Morotai in the Moluccas.

Simultaneously, a US Army-Naval-Marine force under Admiral Chester Nimitz, the dual Commander-in-Chief US Pacific Fleet and Commander-in-Chief Pacific Ocean Areas, moved westwards from Pearl Harbor behind a screen of aircraft carriers. In doing so, he cut right across the line of Tokyo's sea communications in the south and central Pacific which connected the many territories that the Japanese forces had occupied during the first year of the war.

The system pursued was one of 'leap-frogging' over non-essential islands, to land on islands or land areas considered to be of greater strategic importance either as bases or for the defence of Allied communications, even though some of the intervening islands were strongly-held by the enemy. Such a policy was only possible because the Allies had achieved both aerial and naval superiority across most of the Pacific.

By the autumn of 1944, Nimitz had seized the Gilbert Islands, the Marshall Islands and the Marianas, as well as the airfields of the West Carolinas and anchorages where his supporting ships could find replenishment and shelter. Meanwhile, MacArthur, from his southern bases, had reached a point where he was at last in a position to launch an invasion of the Philippines. This was an important step – not only for MacArthur who, in 1942, had famously promised to return, but for the US commanders who considered it essential for the success of their plans to eliminate the enemy's land-based air forces in the Philippines which were regarded as too powerful to by-pass.

The naval force which would carry MacArthur's 6th Army on to the landing beaches of the Philippines was Admiral Thomas Kinkaid's Seventh Fleet. The dominance that the Allies had achieved in the Pacific was such that it allowed Nimitz to release his main force, that of Admiral William F. 'Bull' Halsey's Third Fleet, to support MacArthur's Philippine operations.

BATTLE OF LEYTE GULF

The recapture of the Philippines was expected to be a prolonged and costly endeavour, beginning with the occupation of the most southerly of the Philippine islands, Mindanao. From there MacArthur intended to work his way up to the principal island of the group, Luzon, and the ultimate objective of Manila.

As it happened, on 12 and 13 September 1944, Halsey launched a series of air strikes from his carrier-based aircraft at the Japanese airfields on Luzon. These missions were undertaken in support of operations against Peleliu in the Palau Islands. His aircraft achieved astonishing results. For the loss of nine machines, his men shot down 173 enemy aircraft, destroyed a further 305 on the ground and sank at least fifty-nine ships.

Just as significant was the information he received from a pilot who, operating from the carrier USS *Hornet*, had been shot down over the island of Leyte, which, located in the Visayas group of islands, is the eighth largest island in the Philippines by land area. Rescued by Filipino natives, this airman was subsequently returned to his ship, where he reported that there were no Japanese on Leyte itself.

Reconnaissance flights undertaken by the Third Fleet seem to confirm this, the crews discovering what appeared to be abandoned airstrips. If, indeed, this was the case, then Mindanao could be safely 'leap-frogged' and the entire Philippine enterprise advanced by many weeks, allowing other minor preliminary operations to be cancelled altogether.

Halsey sent word of this to Nimitz, suggesting that the existing operational >>>

Right: General Douglas MacArthur, Supreme Commander, Allied Forces, Southwest Pacific Area, pointing with his pipe on a map of the Pacific, and Admiral Chester W. Nimitz, Commander-in-Chief, Pacific, discuss strategy at MacArthur's headquarters in 1944. (USNHHC)

INTRODUCTION

BATTLE OF LEYTE GULF

schedule should be scrapped, and plans put in place for a direct landing on Leyte instead. There was little hesitation from Nimitz who was present with the leading Allied military and naval figures at the Quebec Conference which was headlined by President Roosevelt and Winston Churchill.

MacArthur's approval of the new plan was, of course, essential. But this was quickly forthcoming, and the Joint Chiefs of Staff began planning for an amphibious assault upon Leyte Island on 20 October 1944.

Few doubted the importance of the landings that were about to be made. 'The Leyte operation was to be the crucial battle of the war in the Pacific,' notes one official US history.[1] 'On its >>>

INTRODUCTION

Above: A group of senior US Navy officers of the Third and Seventh Fleets pictured whilst attending a meeting at Seventh Fleet Headquarters to plan the invasion of Leyte. Pictured from left to right are: Vice Admiral Theodore S. Wilkinson, Commander Amphibious Force, Third Fleet; Vice Admiral Thomas C. Kinkaid, Commander Seventh Fleet; and Rear Admiral Daniel E. Barbey, Commander Amphibious Force, Seventh Fleet. (USNHHC)

Opposite: Admiral Nimitz, centre, greets Admiral William F. Halsey, on board USS *New Jersey* which was the latter's flagship at the Battle of Leyte Gulf. (USNHHC)

BATTLE OF LEYTE GULF

INTRODUCTION

outcome would depend the fate of the Philippines and the future course of the war against Japan ... Leyte was the focal point where the Southwest Pacific forces of General MacArthur were to converge with the Central Pacific forces of Admiral Nimitz in a mighty assault to wrest the Philippines from the hands of the enemy.

'With Leyte under General MacArthur's control, the other islands would be within effective striking distance of his ground and air forces. Leyte was to be the anvil against which he would hammer the Japanese into submission in the central Philippines, the springboard from which he would proceed to the conquest of Luzon for the final attack against Japan itself. Military necessity demanded that the Allies achieve a decisive victory on Leyte. General MacArthur and Admiral Nimitz were committed to employ the maximum resources at their command.'

*

The Seventh Fleet, with its six elderly battleships, sixteen escort carriers, four >>>

Left: In advance of the Leyte invasion, on 10 October 1944, four US carrier task groups (with more than 1,000 aircraft) of Halsey's Third Fleet undertook massive air strikes on Okinawa and the Ryukyu Islands, followed by strikes on Formosa. The strikes caused the Japanese to prematurely execute the air portion of their *Sho* ('Victory') plan for the decisive battle of the war. In the huge air battles that followed, approximately 500 Japanese aircraft were shot down or destroyed on the ground. The loss of these aircraft had profound impact on the subsequent Battle of Leyte Gulf, as the Japanese surface strike groups were deprived of air cover during the battle. Here a Curtiss SB2C-3 Helldiver operating from the carrier USS *Hancock* is pictured flying along the eastern coast of Formosa during the pre-emptive raids undertaken by the Third Fleet on 13 October. (USNHHC)

BATTLE OF LEYTE GULF

heavy cruisers, four light cruisers and ten escorts, was to escort the invasion convoy and then standby off the coast of Leyte to protect MacArthur's force as it disembarked not just its fighting men, but all their supplies and equipment. This would take many days, initially to overcome any resistance should enemy opposition be encountered, and subsequently to ensure the island was secured. Leyte would be the springboard from which the rest of the Philippines would be recaptured, so Kincaid's fleet could expect to be tied down in Philippine waters for many months and would be highly vulnerable to an attack by the enemy.

Halsey's task was, therefore, to ensure that operations of the Seventh Fleet were not impeded by the Imperial Japanese Navy. The Third Fleet's main strike force was that of Task Force 38 under Admiral Marc Mitscher. It, in turn, consisted of four task groups which averaged twenty-three ships – which, generally speaking, amounted to two large carriers, two light carriers, two new battleships, three cruisers, and around fourteen destroyers. **>>>**

Opposite: Admiral Soemu Toyoda, Commander-in-Chief Japanese Combined Fleet, aboard the cruiser *Ōyodo* in September 1944. (USNHHC)

Below: A small number of Royal Australian Navy ships under the command of Commodore Collins, formed part of the Seventh Fleet, including the heavy cruisers *Australia* and *Shropshire*, the destroyers *Arunta* and *Warramunga*, the infantry landing ships *Westralia*, *Kanimbla* and *Manoora*, plus the frigate *Gascoyne*. Shown here is HMAS *Australia*. (USNHHC)

The US warships were to secure air supremacy over the Philippines and, as stated, to cover and protect the Seventh Fleet. But Nimitz also gave Halsey another purpose: 'In case opportunity for destruction of major portions of the enemy fleet offers or can be created, such destruction becomes the primary task.' This certainly got Halsey's attention, as he subsequently wrote to Nimitz: 'My goal is the same as yours – to completely annihilate the Jap fleet if the opportunity offers.'

That opportunity would soon present itself, for Admiral Soemu Toyoda, Commander-in-Chief of the Japanese Combined Fleet, aimed to try and disrupt the American landings in a do-or-die mission involving the whole of his fleet. 'If things went well, we might obtain unexpectedly good results,' Toyoda later explained, 'but if the worst should happen, there was a chance that we would lose the entire fleet. But I felt that that chance had to be taken ....

'Should we lose in the Philippines operations, even though the fleet should be left, the shipping lane to the south would be completely cut off, so that the fleet, if it should come back to Japanese waters, could not obtain its fuel supply. If it should remain in southern waters, it could not receive supplies of ammunition and arms. There would be no sense in saving the fleet at the expense of the Philippines.'[2]

The opposing fleets were determined to fight in a winner-takes-all clash which would be the largest naval battle in history.

Chapter 1

THE LEYTE LANDINGS

The first landings to mark the liberation of the Philippines were made on three small islands which guarded the eastern approaches to Leyte Gulf. 'Despite cyclonic storms and heavy seas,' noted MacArthur's General Staff, 'elements of the 6th Ranger Battalion, augmented by one company of the 21st Infantry, went ashore on Suluan and Dinagat Islands on 17 October 1944. Heavy mists shrouded their approach and they were opposed only by the rough surf and battering winds. Homonhon Island was occupied the next day.'[3]

All three islands were quickly cleared of their small enemy garrisons and radio installations. At the same time, mine sweepers and demolition teams co-operated to sweep the waters and the beaches of all obstacles potentially dangerous to the main operation.

Above: At 08.00 hours on 17 October 1944, the light cruiser USS *Denver* was the first to open fire on a Japanese-held island, Suluan Island, at the entrance to Leyte Gulf. At the time, *Denver* was acting in support of a US Army Ranger operation to seize enemy-held positions covering the approaches to Leyte. (USNHHC)

BATTLE OF LEYTE GULF

THE LEYTE LANDINGS

On 20 October 1944, the largest armada of naval assault craft and warships ever concentrated in the Pacific sailed boldly into Leyte Gulf itself. The landing beaches and tactically important rear areas had already been softened by a continuous two-day ship and aircraft bombardment. After an additional morning barrage, the landing troops were ready to go ashore.

The main assault on the east coast of Leyte began at 10.00 hours in the morning of what was referred to as A-Day. Landings were duly made along an eighteen-mile front between the two small villages of Dulag and San Jose. X Corps, comprising the 1st Cavalry and the 24th Divisions, covered the right flank of the landings to the north; XXIV Corps, consisting of the 7th and 96th Divisions, secured the left flank.

With Japanese opposition at the landing beaches negligible, the US forces were able to advance and by the middle of the afternoon the men of the 1st Cavalry Division, supported by tanks, had secured Tacloban airfield, the most important of the early objectives. For MacArthur, this meant that he was now able to fulfil the promise he had made way back in the dark days of 1942.

Opposite: The action by USS *Denver* was followed by minesweeping operations and, on 18 October, the battleship USS *Pennsylvania* and two cruisers commenced bombardment of the southern Leyte beaches. *Pennsylvania* was armed with twelve 14-inch guns mounted three to a turret – and it is these guns that can be seen here firing on Leyte on 20 October. (USNHHC)

Below: As preparations for the landings intensified, during the afternoon of 18 October the destroyer-transport USS *Goldsborough* was participating in the shore-bombardment of concealed Japanese positions at Dulag in an effort to provide covering fire for underwater demolition teams that were heading for the shore. During this task she was straddled by two 75mm shells, before a third hit her No.1 stack. Two members of the crew were killed and a further sixteen wounded. (USNHHC)

BATTLE OF LEYTE GULF

Right: Part of the Leyte landing force at sea as it bears down upon the Philippines. As the original caption states, "it's tenting tonight in the old Pacific' as this Coast Guard-manned LST moves toward the Philippines under a mighty shield of American sea-power. Tarpaulins are used to pitch crude shelters on the deck, packed with trucks and fighting equipment. Under these shelters, the battle-bound troops and Coast Guardsmen escape the hot quarters below decks.' (US Coast Guard Archives)

Above: Just after midnight on 19 October, the destroyer USS *Ross* was covering the minesweepers when she struck a mine in the swept channel, followed soon after by a second. Although badly damaged, with twenty-three of her crew killed, *Ross* gained the distinction of being the only destroyer in the Pacific to survive hitting two mines in quick succession.

Taken onboard USS *Pennsylvania* four days later, this picture depicts the burial at sea for one of those killed on *Ross* by the mines. (National Museum of the US Navy)

Above: As H-Hour approached on 20 October, the main US invasion fleet entered Leyte Gulf and commenced the amphibious assault by General Douglas MacArthur's Sixth Army on the designated northern and southern beaches. Here, a convoy of Landing Craft, Infantry (LCI) can be seen approaching Leyte just before the landings, the waters in the Gulf being 'glassy calm'. (USNHHC)

Opposite: An aerial view of the landing craft running for the shore, giving some indication of the scale of the amphibious operation. Initial Japanese resistance to the Leyte landings was relatively light, and most of the Japanese ground troops on the island were out of position and soon to be overwhelmed by the massive force about to be put ashore, ultimately totalling some 200,000 US Army troops. (USNHHC)

Below: The destroyer USS *Hutchins* pictured bombarding the beach on 20 October, during the initial landings. (USNHHC)

BATTLE OF LEYTE GULF

Above: US Coast Guard-manned landing craft, loaded with troops, sweep towards the beaches of Leyte Island at H-Hour on 20 October. The men being carried ashore are watching the drama unfolding overhead as American and Japanese engage in combat. (National Museum of the US Navy)

Opposite: An aircraft is shown here endeavouring to lay a smoke screen on the right flank of the invasion beach, as the first waves of landing craft come ashore. (USNHHC)

Main image: These LCVPs running for the beach are from the USS *J. Franklin Bell*, which was a Harris-class attack transport ship. (USNHHC)

THE LEYTE LANDINGS

Above: Gunboats LCI(G)-659 and LCI(G)-461 also laid smoke to help conceal the advancing landing craft. (USNHHC)

Opposite: LVTs bring men and equipment ashore on Leyte on 20 October. The largest single deployment of LVTs by US forces in the Second World War was during the landings at Leyte, with a total of nine Amtrac and two Amtank battalions being employed by the US 6th Army. (US Coast Guard Archives)

Below: The first wave of assault troops hits the beach during the Leyte landings, in this case troops from the LCVPs deployed by the USS *J. Franklin Bell*. Once the men were ashore, the LCVPs quickly turned around and headed back to the attack transport ship to collect the second wave. (USNHHC)

Above: Within an hour of landing, units in most sectors had secured beachheads large enough and deep enough to receive heavy vehicles and large amounts of supplies. Here stores and equipment are being landed on Leyte from a Landing Craft, Vehicle, Personnel (LCVP), also known as a Higgins boat, from the transport vessel USS *Leonard Wood*. (US Navy)

Opposite: Compared to other island assaults in the Pacific Campaign, the Leyte landings were significantly less bloody, but the assault would soon bog down, in large part due to abysmal weather, and it would take a long time for the soggy airfield at Tacloban to become fully operational and enable land-based Army aircraft to take over from Navy aircraft carriers. Here, Boatswain's Mate 2nd Class Robert Driscoll USN, raises the first American flag on the Leyte Beaches. (USNHHC)

BATTLE OF LEYTE GULF

Main Image: US landing craft, as well as the larger LSM-23 and LST-204 (nearest camera), unloading on the beach at Leyte, 20 October 1944. (USNHHC)

THE LEYTE LANDINGS

BATTLE OF LEYTE GULF

THE LEYTE LANDINGS

Main image: A Grumman TBF Avenger patrolling over the landing beaches near Tacloban during the initial landings on 20 October. (USNHHC)

BATTLE OF LEYTE GULF

Main image: A Landing Craft Rockets, or LCI-R, firing on targets ashore during the landings on Leyte, 20 October 1944. (USNHHC)

THE LEYTE LANDINGS

Above: As the US landings on Leyte continued, it did not take long for Japanese aerial counter-attacks to begin, although the reduced number of aircraft available to defend the Philippines, thanks to Halsey's earlier strikes, made them less effective than they might otherwise have been. Nevertheless, on the afternoon of the 20 October, a Japanese torpedo plane succeed in hitting the light cruiser USS *Honolulu*, shown here, with one torpedo. Sixty of *Honolulu*'s crew were killed, and though the ship did not sink, she played no further part in the war. *Honolulu* is pictured here beached off Leyte, with a fleet tug alongside, on 21 October 1944. (US Navy)

Opposite page: A US war dog and its handler shelter in a hastily dug foxhole or crater on one of the landing beaches on Leyte during 20 October 1944. One of those who recalled the events that day was Alva Smith, a former Private 1st Class in the 96th Division who was wounded in the landings: 'They were dropping a lot of mortar [shells] on us. I remember saying to myself "What the hell am I doing here?"'. (US Coast Guard Archives)

BATTLE OF LEYTE GULF

THE LEYTE LANDINGS

Main image: Organisation of the passage of men and vehicles across the landing beaches was in the hands of the US Navy and here we can see a Navy beach control unit setting up a communication base. (USNHHC)

Left: The destroyer USS *Cony* laying a smoke screen, to protect shipping off Leyte from Japanese air attack on 20 October, pictured from the battleship USS *West Virginia*. (USNHHC)

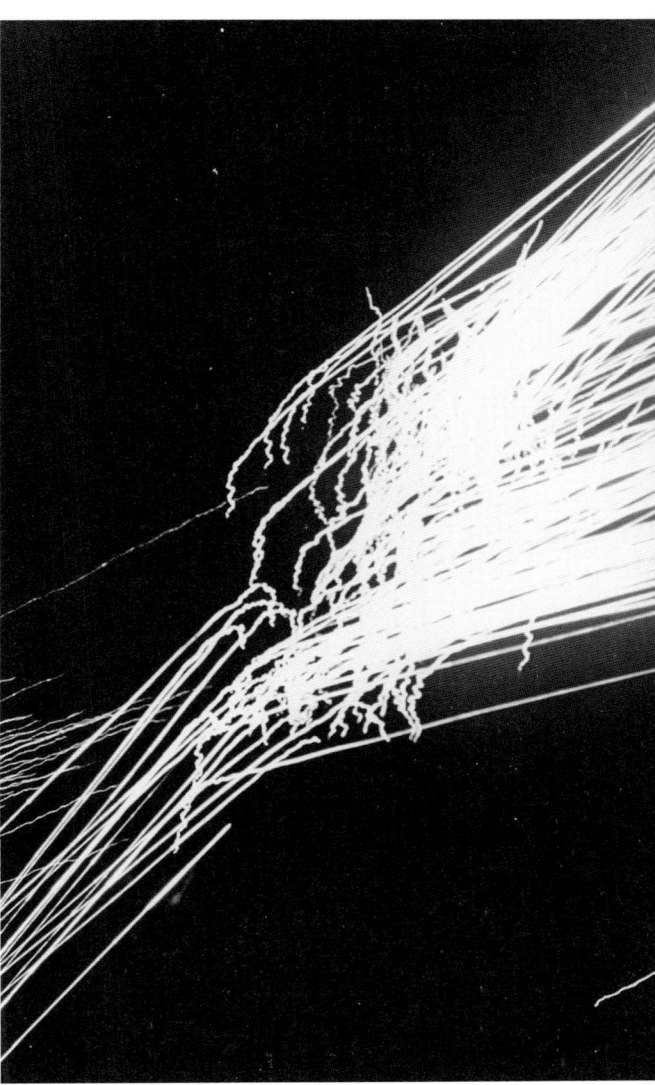

Above: Nightfall on 20 October brought no respite from the Japanese aircraft and here 40mm tracer rounds from USS *Pennsylvania*, and other ships, can be seen converging on a Japanese plane during an attack on Allied shipping. (USNHHC)

Above: Meanwhile, the invasion continued on the 21st, as did the Japanese attacks, and at 06.00 hours, an Aichi D3A dive-bomber slammed into the foremast of the County-class heavy cruiser HMAS *Australia*. Although most of the aircraft fell overboard, the bridge and forward superstructure were showered with debris and burning fuel. Thirty men were killed, including Captain Emile Dechaineux DSC, and a further sixty-one injured. The damage inflicted in the collision can be seen here.

In this picture note the US Mk.4 fire control radar antenna atop the gun director on *Australia*'s starboard bridge wing, and the British-type twin 4-inch anti-aircraft gun on the main deck. (USNHHC)

Right: The bridge of HMAS *Australia* in September 1944, just before sailing to take part in the Leyte landings. It was this area of the cruiser that was damaged in the kamikaze attack on 21 October 1944. Captain Emile Dechaineux DSC, in the white uniform facing right, was among those killed.

Although it is stated in the official history of the Royal Australian Navy that HMAS *Australia* was therefore the first Allied ship to be hit by a kamikaze attack, other sources disagree, noting that it was not a pre-planned strike, but undertaken at the pilot's own initiative. Whatever the full circumstances, HMAS *Australia* took no further part in the Leyte operations but was able to return to service in December. (Courtesy of the Australian War Memorial; 017623)

Below: The destroyer USS *Humphreys* shown here supporting operations off Leyte on 21 October. Having transported the personnel of Underwater Demolition Team No.5 to the Leyte beaches on 18 October, *Humphreys* remained to provide fire support and guard against Japanese submarines, which she did until the 21st. Having assisted in shooting down a Japanese bomber on the 21st, she sailed from Leyte, in a convoy, the same day. (USNHHC)

BATTLE OF LEYTE GULF

Main image: The operation to capture Leyte and then the rest of the Philippines was a huge undertaking, with every shell, spare part, and morsel of food required having to be carried in ships from either the West Coast of America or Australia. Fuel and lubricants were sourced from the USA and the West Indies. Ammunition arrived from the USA via Australia. A third of all fresh produce came from the USA, the rest from Australia. This required a massive fleet train to carry the necessary supplies. For this enormous logistical effort, Task Group 30.8 of the Third Fleet, which augmented the Seventh Fleet support force, comprised thirty-four oilers, eleven escort carriers, nineteen destroyers and twenty-six destroyer escorts.

This is a view of a supply depot on one of the Leyte's beaches on 21 October. It provides an indication of the huge logistical task faced by the US Navy to keep the ground forces supplied. (USNHHC)

BATTLE OF LEYTE GULF

Above: An historic moment captured on camera. Soon after the main landings on Leyte and following close behind the assault echelons, General Douglas MacArthur and his staff, accompanied by Philippine president Sergio Osmeña, wades through the surf, in what one account describes as drenching rain, to step ashore on the muddy stretch of Red Beach near Palo.

This image was taken by MacArthur's personal photographer, Gaetano Faillace. It has often been stated that the picture was staged, but the CBS correspondent William J. Dunn, who was present during the landing and is the only one in the picture not wearing a helmet or hat, has declared that this claim 'is one of the most ludicrous misconceptions to come out of that war'.

Organised resistance came to an end on Leyte on 31 December, but individual Japanese soldiers continued to hold out until May 1945. (NARA)

Opposite page: This photograph of General MacArthur, nonchalantly puffing on his legendary corncob pipe, was taken by a Coast Guard combat photographer as the American commander surveyed the Leyte Island beachhead. To the right of MacArthur is the Philippine president Sergio Osmeña.

The area where MacArthur stepped ashore is today part of the 16.8 acre site that forms the MacArthur Leyte Landing Memorial National Park. A key feature of the park is a set of seven bronze statues that, overlooking a shallow pool, depict MacArthur and his entourage as they stepped ashore on A-Day. As well as MacArthur, they were Sergio Osmeña, Lieutenant General Richard Sutherland, Brigadier General Carlos P. Romulo, Major General Courtney Whitney, Sergeant Francisco Salveron and William J. Dunn. (National Museum of the US Navy)

THE LEYTE LANDINGS

Main Image: General Douglas MacArthur (centre), accompanied by Lieutenant General George C. Kenney, Lieutenant General Richard K. Sutherland and Major General Verne D. Mudge (Commanding General, First Cavalry Division), inspects the beachhead on Leyte Island, 20 October 1944.

Note the crowd of onlookers. The swamped LCVP in the right background is from USS *Ormsby*. (NARA)

Above: General Douglas MacArthur onboard *PT-525* whilst bound for Tacloban, Leyte, to participate in liberation ceremonies on 24 October 1944. Those present are, left to right: Lieutenant Alexander W. Wells, USNR, the captain of *PT-525*; General MacArthur; Commander Selmon S. Bowling, the commanding officer of the Seventh Fleet's Motor Torpedo Boat squadrons; and Lieutenant General Walter Krueger, Commanding General 6th Army. (USNHHC)

BATTLE OF LEYTE GULF

Above: General Douglas MacArthur and his entourage make their way off the beach near Palo during the Leyte landings. Speaking to millions of expectant Filipinos over a portable radio set, MacArthur made a declaration, which included the following:

'This is the Voice of Freedom, General MacArthur speaking. People of the Philippines: I have returned. By the grace of Almighty God our forces stand again on Philippine soil – soil consecrated in the blood of our two peoples. We have come, dedicated and committed to the task of destroying every vestige of enemy control over your daily lives, and of restoring, upon a foundation of indestructible strength, the liberties of your people …

'Rally to me. Let the indomitable spirit of Bataan and Corregidor lead on. As the lines of battle roll forward to bring you within the zone of operations, rise and strike! For future generations of your sons and daughters, strike! In the name of your sacred dead, strike! Let no heart be faint. Let every arm be steeled. The guidance of Divine God points the way. Follow in His name to the Holy Grail of righteous victory!' (National Museum of the US Navy)

Chapter 2

THE JAPANESE NAVAL FORCES

By late 1944, the Imperial Japanese Navy had anticipated, indeed expected, that the Philippines would be the Allies' main target. The Japanese commanders had also concluded that Leyte would be the first island to be attacked and had prepared accordingly. Their plan to defend the Philippines – initially Operation *Shō-Gō 1* but later modified to become *Shō-Gō 2* after the loss of so many aircraft during Halsey's strikes on Formosa and Okinawa – involved three separate forces.

Above: Japanese battleships of the 'First Diversion Strike Force', more commonly referred to as the 'Centre Force', pictured anchored at Brunei, Borneo, in October 1944, just prior to the Battle of Leyte Gulf. From left to right they are *Musashi*, *Yamato*, a cruiser and *Nagato*.

It was upon receiving news of the Allied landings at Leyte that this force had moved to Brunei, where the ships took on fuel and then divided into two parts. The major portion of the force remained under the command of Kurita, and included the super-battleships *Yamato* and *Musashi*, along with the battleships *Nagato*, *Kongo* and *Haruna*, ten heavy cruisers, two light cruisers and fifteen destroyers. (USNHHC)

Overall command was exercised by Admiral Soemu Toyoda (who replaced Admiral Mineichi Koga after he was killed in a plane crash in March 1944) as commander of the Japanese Combined Fleet. Toyoda, in effect the opposite number to Admiral Nimitz, moved ashore in Japan from his flagship, the light cruiser *Ōyodo*, before the battle so that he could have better communications capability to command the battle.

The first of Toyoda's three forces was the First Mobile Fleet, referred to as the 'Main Body' in Japanese communications which confused the US commanders, which is more often called the 'Northern Force'. This fleet was under the command of Vice Admiral Jisaburo Ozawa, the senior Japanese commander in tactical command of the battle. This force was essentially what remained of the First Mobile Fleet after the Battle of the Philippine Sea. It included the fleet carrier *Zuikaku*, the last surviving carrier of the Pearl Harbor strike force, the light carrier *Zuiho*, and the converted seaplane tenders *Chitose* and *Chiyoda*, with only about 110 aircraft between all four carriers.

Added to the force were the recently converted 'hybrid' battleships *Ise* and *Hyūga*, each of which had their aft two main battery turrets replaced with a flight deck, but which deployed without aircraft. Three light cruisers and nine destroyers provided the escort.

The 'First Diversion Strike Force', which was intended to be the primary strike force, was usually referred to as the 'Centre Force' or just 'First Striking Force'. Under the command of Vice Admiral Takeo Kurita, this force initially consisted of seven battleships, eleven heavy cruisers, two light cruisers, and escorting destroyers, which were based near Singapore to be near fuel supplies (which were already severely depleted in Japan due to submarine attacks on tankers).

The third Japanese force, referred to as the Southern Force, was under the command of Vice

Below: The Centre Force seen here leaving Brunei Bay, Borneo, on 22 October 1944, en route to the Philippines.

The ships visible here are, from right to left, the battleships *Nagato*, *Musashi* and *Yamato*, plus the heavy cruisers *Maya*, *Chokai*, *Takao*, *Atago*, *Haguro* and *Myoko*. (USNHHC)

Admiral Shoji Nishimura. This comprised the elderly battleships *Fusō* and *Yamashiro*, as well as the heavy cruiser *Mogami* and four destroyers. Attached to the Southern Force was a subsidiary division, sometimes called the Second Striking Force. Under the command of Vice Admiral Kiyohide Shima, this force consisted of the heavy cruisers *Nachi* and *Ashigara*, a light cruiser, and four destroyers. This body was originally, the Japanese Fifth Fleet which was responsible for the defence of northern Japan.

*

It was on the day after the start of the Allied operations at Leyte, 21 October, that, news of the landings having reached Tokyo, the Japanese Chief of the Naval Staff issued a directive for 'urgent operations'. Operation *Shō-Gō 2* had been given the go-ahead.

The aim of this operation was for the Task Force Main Body – the Northern Force – to sortie from Japan and approach the Philippines from the north, stationing itself off the island of Luzon. This body, composed mainly of aircraft carriers but with few actual aircraft on board, would act as the 'bait', drawing the US covering forces – Halsey's Third Fleet – away from protecting the landing force. Once the Third Fleet had been enticed away from Leyte, Vice Admiral Shōji Nishimura's Second Striking Force, the Southern Force, would then bear down on Leyte which it was hoped would draw off Kincaid's Seventh Fleet. With the landing ships then unprotected, Vice Admiral Takeo Kurita's First Striking Force, the Centre Force, would easily be able to swoop in and destroy the landing craft, leaving the Allied troops stranded until a counter-invasion could be launched to wipe them out.

But that, or something like it, was what Admiral 'Bull' Halsey was hoping for. He expected the Japanese to make a serious attempt to disrupt the landings and that would give him the chance to wipe out what remained of the Japanese naval forces.

Below: *Musashi* shown here leaving Brunei on 22 October with the rest of Kurita's Centre Force. *Musashi* was one of just three *Yamato*-class ships, which were the heaviest and most powerfully armed battleships ever constructed, displacing almost 73,000 tons fully loaded and armed with nine 18.1 inch (46cm) main guns.

Above: A 14-inch gun being installed in No.3 turret of *Hyūga*, the second, and last, of the Ise-class of battleships which were built at the end of the First World War. *Hyūga* was part of the 'Northern Force'

Opposite page top: A photograph of the battleship *Musashi* taken from the from the forward superstructure in June 1942.

Opposite page bottom: The heavy cruiser *Mogami* shown here in happier times, shortly after commissioning in 1935.

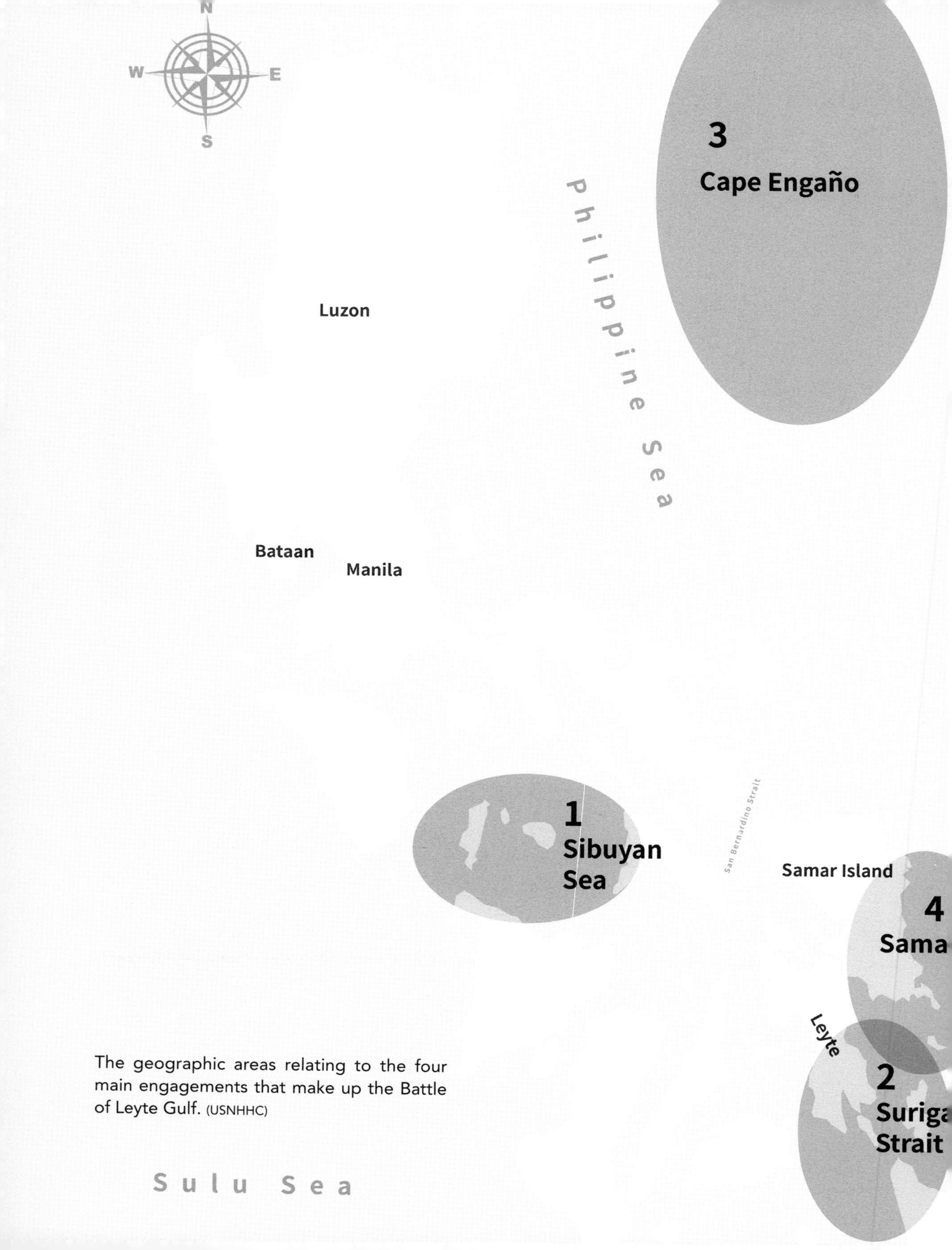

3 Cape Engaño

Luzon

Philippine Sea

Bataan   Manila

1 Sibuyan Sea

San Bernardino Strait

Samar Island

4 Samar

Leyte

2 Surigao Strait

The geographic areas relating to the four main engagements that make up the Battle of Leyte Gulf. (USNHHC)

Sulu Sea

Chapter 3

BATTLE OF THE SIBUYAN SEA

24 October 1944

In order that early warning might be had of the approach of any hostile naval forces, US submarines had been stationed to patrol to a radius of 1,000 miles to the north and east of the Philippines. At the same time, carrier task forces of the Third Fleet and air searches by Central Pacific forces from Palau and Saipan were depended upon to give early information of the approach of enemy forces east of the Philippines.

Above: USS *Dace* at the New London submarine base, Groton, Connecticut, on 23 July 1943, the day she was placed in commission. (USNHHC)

Above: USS *Darter* aground on Bombay Shoal, off southwest Palawan. Note damage caused by her crew's attempts to scuttle her. (USNHHC)

It was the submarines which first raised the alarm. At 02.00 hours on 23 October 1944, Commander David Hayward McClintock of the USS *Darter*, which was operating with its sister submarine, USS *Dace*, reported that he had made radar contact with three Japanese battleships making 15 knots to the south-west of Palawan Island. It was one of the most important messages of the war in the Pacific. Until that moment, the Americans had no idea where the Japanese fleet might be. This was, of course, Admiral Kurita's Centre Force.

On the super-battleship *Yamato*, the radio room intercepted *Darter*'s message to the US fleet and correctly recognized the submarine as being close. Yet, inexplicably, no change whatsoever was made in the Japanese formation or its direction. As a result, the Japanese were entirely unprepared for what happened next.

McClintock fired *Darter*'s first six torpedoes at what was Admiral Kurita's flagship, the heavy cruiser *Atago*. Four of the torpedoes hit the target, ripping open *Atago* from stem to stern. The cruiser capsized and sank in twenty minutes, taking 360 of its crew with it. Among the survivors was Kurita, who, having been forced to jump overboard, managed to stay afloat until, utterly exhausted, he was rescued by a destroyer. He duly transferred his flag to *Yamato*.

It was then *Dace*'s turn, and in its sights was another heavy cruiser, *Maya*. Four torpedoes raced towards *Maya*, and all four smashed into the cruiser's port side. Convulsed with primary and secondary explosions, she sank with 336 men still on board, including her captain. The two submarines then withdrew. *Darter* ran aground and had to be abandoned, but her crew were taken off by *Dace*.

Kurita's Central Force was spotted a second time during the 23rd by the submarine USS *Angler*. Also, another report was received from the submarine *Bream* of a large force to the west of Luzon, and of elements of possibly another force – the as yet unidentified Southern Force – south of Negros Island. The great battle that Admiral Halsey sought was almost upon him.

Kurita's ships were tracked by a single reconnaissance aircraft throughout the night of 23/24th and, at dawn on the 24th, this was increased to eight aircraft. None of those aircraft were sent to search to the north of Luzon, consequently the Northern Force remained unknown to Halsey, despite its deliberate efforts to be detected, intentionally breaking radio silence with messages that, inexplicably, US radio intelligence failed to intercept.

Also inexplicable was Halsey's decision on 22 October to allow Vice Admiral John S. McCain's Task Group 38.1 – the strongest of the carrier groups – to sail to the fleet base at Ulithi in the Caroline Islands, some 1,800 miles away, to provision and rearm. He had sent both McCain's and Rear Admiral R.E. Davison's Task Group 38.4 to Ulithi, but when *Darter*'s message was received, Halsey recalled Davison but permitted McCain to continue to the Caroline Islands. Halsey eventually recalled McCain on 24 October, and though TG 38.1 raced back at 30 knots, the most powerful American carrier group was still more than a day's steaming away when the battle began, leaving the Third Fleet effectively shorn of nearly 40 per cent of its air strength for most of the engagement.

Upon receiving word that Admiral Toyoda's Centre Force had entered the Sibuyan Sea, Halsey ordered his aircraft to launch at 08.33 hours on the 24th, with one simple instruction: 'Strike! Repeat: Strike!'

Over the course of the day, they did just that, mercilessly pounding the Japanese Centre Force with bombs and torpedoes while fending off incoming waves of Japanese aircraft launched from Luzon and other parts of the Philippines. However, Rear Admiral Frederick Sherman, commanding Task Force 38.3 in the fleet carrier USS *Essex*, picked up a report of a large Japanese force – the Southern Force – south of Mindoro Island, and he immediately issued orders to his aircraft to prepare an attack upon this enemy group. But before his aircraft could launch, enemy shore-based aircraft were detected approaching from Luzon.

Vice Admiral Takijiro Onishi, commander of land-based Japanese naval aircraft ashore in the Philippines (mostly on Luzon), launched three waves of aircraft of about fifty to sixty planes each at US carriers operating east of Luzon, with Task Group 38.3 the closest target. At 09.50 hours, the first of these waves was detected on radar approaching the US carriers. Many of the carriers' aircraft were already airborne on their way to Luzon to attack airfields, leaving a reduced number of fighters for fleet defence. Sherman quickly scrambled six F6F Hellcat fighters from *Essex* as the Japanese approached to twenty-two nautical miles from the carriers. Several of the fighters, including one flown by Air Group Fifteen's commander, Commander David McCampbell, were launched without a full load of fuel.

At this point, another large body of Japanese aircraft – Onishi's second wave – was detected, and every available fighter was sent up by *Essex*, the other fleet carrier *Lexington* and the light carriers *Princeton* and *Langley*. Soon, an enormous aerial battle raged in the skies.

Despite such heroics, disaster was to strike Sherman's group. After about ninety minutes of combat, there was a lull in the fighting and the fighters, low on fuel and ammunition, landed back on the carriers. The radar screens showed no signs of enemy aircraft but, unnoticed amid the returning American aircraft, was a lone Yokosuka D4Y Suisei 'Judy' dive bomber. It appeared out of low cloud and dropped a single bomb on *Princeton*. It would prove fatal; *Princeton* was subsequently abandoned and later sunk by torpedoes.

BATTLE OF LEYTE GULF

Though the loss of *Princeton* was a blow to Task Group 38.3, the Japanese attack from Luzon cost them a staggering 150 aircraft shot down by the defending fighters and anti-aircraft fire from the warships. Halsey's strike aircraft had also caught Kurita's Centre Force in the Sibuyan Sea and endeavoured to exact revenge, mounting six waves of attacks that continued throughout the day.

At 10.30 hours, aircraft from USS *Intrepid* and USS *Cabot*, part of Task Group 38.2, struck first. Cloud cover at 5-6,000 feet hampered the crews somewhat, but there was no air opposition, though anti-aircraft fire was reported to have been 'intense'. In all, a total of around 300 sorties (figures vary) were flown from the US carriers during the 24th. The results from such an enormous effort were, perhaps, a little disappointing, considering the Japanese warships were devoid of any aerial protection. Although the pilots made remarkable claims, in reality, Kurita lost only *Musashi* and *Myōkō*. The Japanese Admiral, however, turned his fleet to the west to get out of range of the American aircraft.

In light of what appeared to be a retrograde move by Kurita and the claims of his returning pilots, Halsey assumed that the Centre Force had been driven off and, at least for the time being, could be ignored. But Kurita was far from beaten and at 17.15 hours he turned around again and headed for the San Bernardino Strait. The latter was a strait in >>>

Right: Pilots of Torpedo Squadron 13 (VT-13) in their ready room aboard USS *Franklin*, 24 October 1944, just before the Battle of the Sibuyan Sea. They are watching as the position of the Japanese fleet is posted. Note the life preservers, with die marker pouches, worn by several of the men. VT-13's Commanding Officer, Lieutenant Commander Larry French, is second from the left, with a navigation board beside his chair. (USNHHC)

BATTLE OF THE SIBUYAN SEA

BATTLE OF LEYTE GULF

Main mage: Scene on the flight deck of *Essex* during the Japanese air attack on 24 October. A Japanese plane is burning on the water in the background. (USNHHC)

BATTLE OF THE SIBUYAN SEA

the Philippines, between the islands of Luzon and Samar, which connects the Samar Sea with the Philippine Sea.

As a precaution, just in case Kurita returned and tried once again to interfere with the Leyte landings, Halsey wanted to be able to respond quickly and block the San Bernardino Strait. He informed his task force commanders that if compelled to send a force into the Strait he would form a temporary task force – Task Force 34 – to deal with that scenario. Unfortunately, the message Halsey sent to his subordinates, timed at 15.12 hours, explaining this was badly worded. The key sentences in the message read: 'FROM TG 38.4 WILL BE FORMED AS TASK FORCE 34 UNDER VICE ADMIRAL LEE, COMMANDER BATTLE LINE. TF 34 TO ENGAGE DECISIVELY AT LONG RANGES.'

This was misinterpreted by Kincaid to mean that Task Force 34 was already formed or was about to be formed and that it was, or would be, covering the San Bernardino Strait. The consequences of Halsey's garbled message would shortly become apparent.

Possibly realising that his message was unclear, Halsey sent a second message which explained his intentions more explicitly: 'IF THE ENEMY SORTIES (THROUGH SAN BERNADINO [sic] STRAIT) TF 34 WILL BE FORMED WHEN DIRECTED BY ME.' But Halsey sent this message by radio not by telecommunication and it never reached Kincaid who was out of range.

Halsey failed to follow this up with written telegraphic confirmation. Consequently, Kincaid was left assuming that a powerful task force was guarding the San Bernardino Strait and that his operations in support of MacArthur's 6th Army could continue unimpeded as before. Tragically, he was wrong.

Right: A number of USS *Essex*'s 20mm anti-aircraft guns in action during the Japanese attack on TF 38 on the 24th. (USNHHC)

BATTLE OF THE SIBUYAN SEA

49

Left: Commander David McCampbell is seen here in the cockpit of his F6F Hellcat fighter on board USS *Essex* on 30 October. The Japanese flags represent his thirty kills by that date, including those from 24 October. That day McCampbell 'intercepted and daringly attacked a formation of sixty hostile land-based craft approaching our forces. Fighting desperately but with superb skill against such overwhelming airpower, he shot down nine Japanese planes and, completely disorganizing the enemy group, forced the remainder to abandon the attack before a single aircraft could reach the Fleet.' These were the words on his citation for the Medal of Honor. With the award of the Navy Cross for his actions the next day, 25 October, McCampbell is the only man ever to earn both of the US Navy's top two awards in successive days. (USNHHC)

Below: The bomb that the lone Yokosuka D4Y Suisei 'Judy' dive bomber dropped on *Princeton* hit and penetrated the flight deck amidships. The carrier's speed was immediately reduced. Such a small bomb striking a 15,000-ton warship should not have been a major cause for concern. But it ignited gasoline in the ship's hangar and a fire rapidly took hold, enveloping the entire hangar. In this image, a damage control party examines *Princeton*'s shattered hangar. (USNHHC)

Above: A closer view of the stricken USS *Princeton*. About twenty minutes after the bomb had hit, there occurred a series of heavy explosions in the hangar. Some of the torpedo warheads in the planes may have detonated or gasoline vapor may have exploded violently. These explosions blew up the flight deck, wrecked both elevators, and forced the evacuation of all machinery spaces. In these images, a damage control party examines *Princeton*'s shattered hangar. (US Navy)

Opposite page top: USS *Princeton* on fire at about 10.04 hours on 24 October. This view shows smoke rising from the ship's second large explosion, as USS *Reno* steams by in the foreground. (NARA)

Opposite page bottom: Black smoke from the fires which raged along her deck was so dense that at times the carrier was completely hidden from view. The escorting destroyers circled round *Princeton*, hosing her with water, but the blaze continued unchecked. She stopped dead in the water and men were seen jumping into the sea to avoid the flames. Around midday, the efforts of the other ships appeared to be having an effect as the fire seemed to be diminishing. This was only temporary, and a couple of hours later, black smoke again shrouded the carrier.

Princeton is seen here on fire, but still underway, about twenty minutes after she was hit, photographed from USS *South Dakota*. (US Navy)

BATTLE OF LEYTE GULF

Main image: The anti-aircraft cruiser USS *Reno* moves alongside the port quarter of the burning *Princeton* to assist in fighting the fires. Five times *Reno* closed *Princeton*, but on each occasion could not remain close in because of intense heat and smoke from the burning carrier. At one point the carrier began listing and her flight deck struck the cruiser, badly damaging one of the 40mm gun positions. (USNHHC)

BATTLE OF THE SIBUYAN SEA

Above: Given the fires burning in *Princeton*, various destroyers made repeated attempts to go alongside and spray water on the flames. Heavy seas frustrated those moves, however, and *Morrison*, *Gatling* and *Irwin* all suffered serious damage in collisions with the heaving carrier. Here one warship is pictured trying to get alongside *Princeton*, as pictured from the USS *Cassin Young*. (National Museum of the US Navy)

Opposite page top: After her sister ships had failed in their attempts, it was decided that the cruiser USS *Birmingham* should move alongside *Princeton* since it was felt she could better withstand any blows. This picture shows *Birmingham* moving alongside the carrier. (National Museum of the US Navy)

Opposite page bottom: A clear indication of the desperate situation onboard *Princeton* can be gauged from this photograph taken from the Fletcher-class destroyer USS *Cassin Young*. (National Museum of the US Navy)

Overleaf: A photograph taken from the foredeck of *Birmingham* as she stood alongside *Princeton* while playing its part in the efforts to quell the fires raging on the carrier. (USNHHC)

BATTLE OF THE SIBUYAN SEA

BATTLE OF LEYTE GULF

Main image: USS *Princeton*'s port forward area, as seen from USS *Birmingham* during attempts to control her fires during the afternoon of 24 October. Note the damage to the carrier's 40mm gun position and catwalk, caused by *Birmingham*'s No.2 6/47 turret when the two ships came together. A flight deck tractor can be seen partially hanging on Princeton's deck edge, whilst F6F and TBM airplanes are parked forward. (USNHHC)

BATTLE OF THE SIBUYAN SEA

BATTLE OF LEYTE GULF

Main image: Crewmen on USS *Birmingham* play firehoses on the burning *Princeton*. Within a short period of time, the light cruiser sent fourteen water hoses and thirty-eight men from her damage control teams over to the carrier. This extra assistance helped extinguish one of the two major fires in the carrier. During the middle of the afternoon, the threat of a Japanese attack forced USS *Birmingham* to pull back. With the danger passed, as she moved back into position disaster struck. (USNHHC)

BATTLE OF LEYTE GULF

Left: At 15.22 hours, just as the light cruiser was moving back alongside the carrier, flames touched off *Princeton*'s after magazines. Some 400 General Purpose bombs then ignited, blowing off the entire stern of *Princeton*. Not an officer or man left on the carrier escaped death or injury. The carnage on board *Birmingham* was little better as steel fragments, wooden planking and all manner of debris raked the cruiser's upper deck, crowded with men trying to fight the fire and manning the anti-aircraft guns, from stem to stern. Half her officers and men were killed or wounded in an instant. 'It is impossible, even remotely, to adequately describe the grisly scene of human fragmentation,' wrote her Executive Officer, who took over command from the severely injured Captain Thomas B. Inglis.[4] (USNHHC)

Below: USS *Birmingham*, on the left, and a destroyer pull away from *Princeton* following the explosion. Only one doctor was available at the time on *Birmingham* and he later wrote of the conduct of the crew: 'I really have no words at my command that can adequately describe the veritable splendour of the conduct of all hands, wounded and unwounded. Men with legs off, arms off, with gaping wounds in their sides, with the tops of their heads furrowed by fragments, would insist, "I'm all right. Take care of Joe over there," or "Don't waste morphine on me, Commander, just hit me over the head". Terrible as the destruction was, it is a source of supreme gratification to know the heights of courage and forgetfulness of self to which one's shipmates can rise.'5 (US Navy)

Right: A close up of the damage to *Birmingham*'s after smokestack and superstructure. The final casualty figure on the cruiser was 229 killed, four missing believed dead, 211 seriously wounded and twenty-five slightly wounded. (NARA)

Below: As *Birmingham*'s surviving crew members battled the situation they faced on the cruiser, continuing efforts by the other warships to save *Princeton* failed and *Reno* and *Irwin* eventually scuttled the burning aircraft carrier with torpedoes in order to permit US forces to clear the area. Seen here is an explosion on the carrier when a torpedo fired by *Reno* struck at 17.50 hours. (USNHHC)

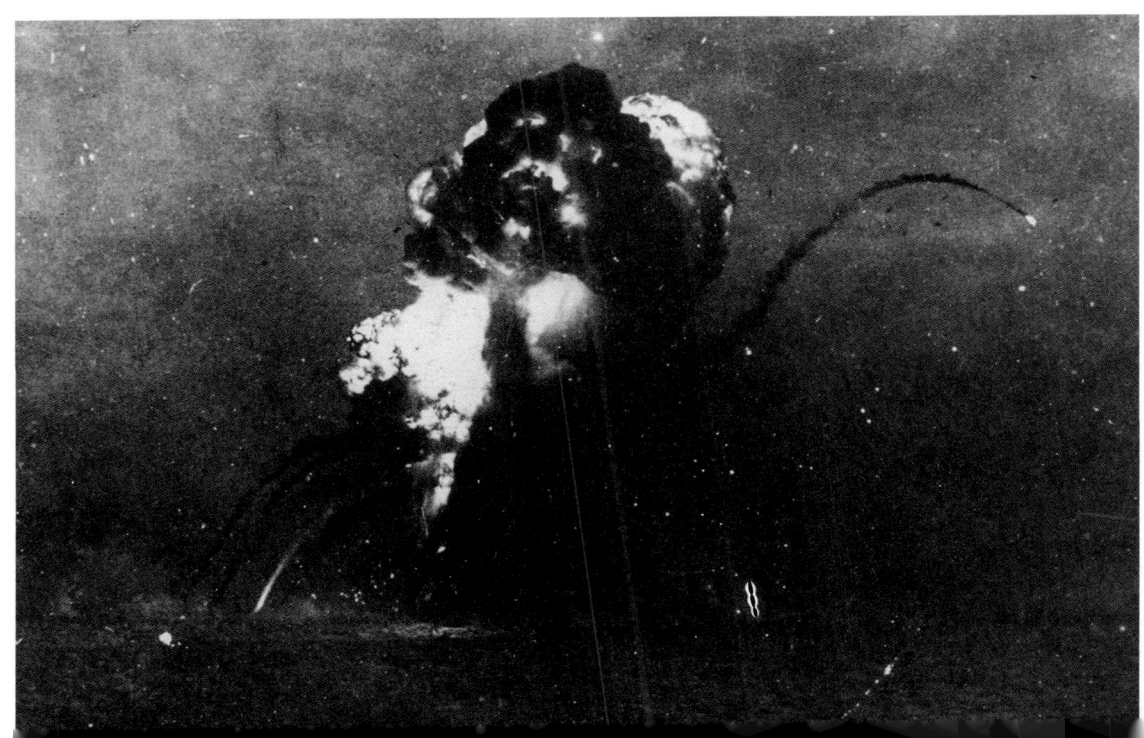

BATTLE OF LEYTE GULF

Main image: The Japanese battleship *Nagato* and a *Nachi*-class cruiser are seen here under attack by aircraft from USS *Intrepid*. During the events of 24 October, *Nagato* was attacked by several groups of US dive bombers and fighters. In one of these assaults, at 14.16 hours, she was hit by bombs dropped by aircraft operating from USS *Franklin* and USS *Cabot*. Whilst the damage was quite extensive, and fifty-two crewmen were killed, the battleship survived the Battle of the Sibuyan Sea.
(USNHHC)

BATTLE OF THE SIBUYAN SEA

Inset: *Nagato* fighting back as she comes under attack on 24 October. (NARA)

Main image: USS *Intrepid* photographed from the rear seat of an SB2C after it had taken off to attack the Japanese Fleet in the Battle of Sibuyan Sea, 24 October 1944. (NARA)

BATTLE OF THE SIBUYAN SEA

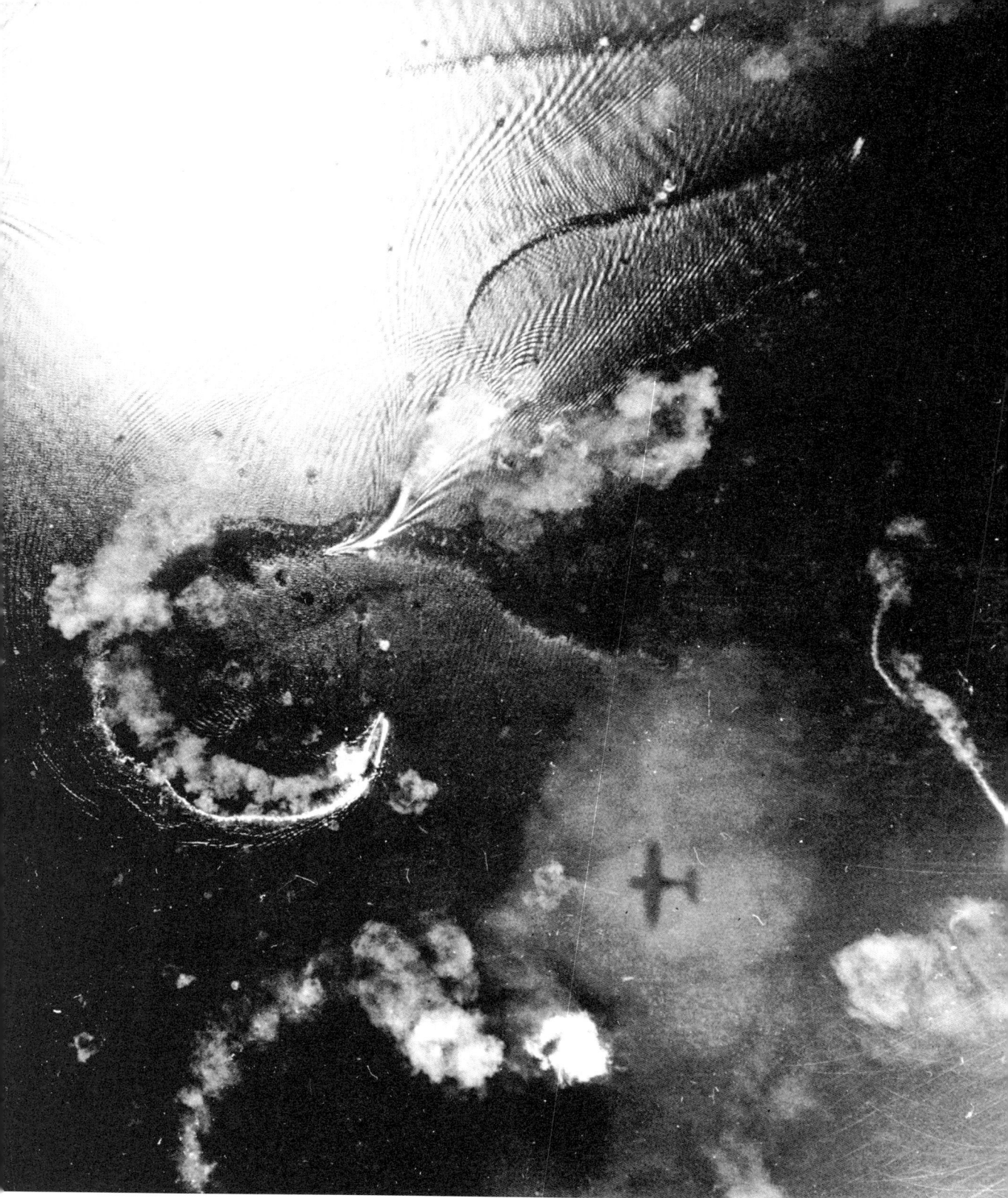

Above: During the US aerial assaults on 24 October, Lieutenant Commander Arthur L. Downing scored two hits from his Curtiss SB2C Helldiver on the battleship *Yamato* as she transited the Sibuyan Sea. This picture, taken by Aviation Radioman Petty Officer (ARM2) 2nd Class John L. Carver, also a Helldiver crewman, shows a bomb striking the battleship near her forward 460mm gun turret after Downing had gone in through intense anti-aircraft fire at low altitude. This hit did not produce serious damage and her battle worthiness was unaffected. (National Museum of the US Navy)

Left: The Japanese battleship *Yamato* (lower centre) and other ships take evasive action while under attack by US Navy carrier-based aircraft in the Sibuyan Sea. The shadow of one aircraft is visible on a cloud in lower right centre. (US Navy)

Right: Lieutenant Commander Arthur L. Downing (on the left) and ARM2 John L. Carver pictured following their return to their carrier, USS *Essex*, after bombing *Yamato* during the Battle of the Sibuyan Sea. (National Museum of the US Navy)

Above: The dramatic scene as a Japanese battleship (at left), either *Yamato* or *Musashi*, and other warships manoeuvre while under attack in the Sibuyan Sea. The warship lower left, as well as the two on the extreme right, are heavy cruisers. (USNHHC)

Below: A Japanese light cruiser, either *Agano* or *Noshiro*, under attack during the Battle of the Sibuyan Sea. (USNHHC)

Above: A second wave of aircraft from USS *Essex*, USS *Lexington* and *Intrepid* also struck, with most hits (about ten) being scored on the super-battleship *Musashi*. Here *Musashi* is shown here under heavy attack from US aircraft during the Battle of the Sibuyan Sea, 24 October 1944. (USNHHC)

Below: Another view of *Musashi* under intense attack on 24 October. Aircraft from *Franklin* hit *Musashi* with eleven bombs and eight torpedoes. (USNHHC)

Above: *Musashi* finally capsized and sank at about 19.30 hours, taking 1,023 of her 2,399 crewmen to the bottom, including 143 survivors of the previously sunk heavy cruiser *Maya*. Rear Admiral Toshihira Inoguchi wrote in his diary: 'Although I intended to fight this battle out to the end, it now seems that we have come to the end of the line. It is 1855. I would like to write down all my thoughts, but it is already dark. In the worse circumstances, we will be forced to remove the portrait of the Emperor, lower the flag, and abandon ship.'[6] Inoguchi went down with his charge. (USNHHC)

Below: The super-battleship *Musashi* down at the bow after being hit by US Navy carrier aircraft in the Sibuyan Sea. The loss of *Musashi*, the pride of the Japanese navy, was a serious psychological blow to Kurita and other Japanese who witnessed it. Eighteen US Navy aircraft were lost in the attacks. (USNHHC)

Above: Safely back on his carrier, Bombing Squadron 13's commanding officer, Lieutenant Charles Skinner (centre), describes his unit's attack on the Japanese fleet in Sibuyan Sea.

Chapter 4

BATTLES OF THE SULU SEA AND THE SURIGAO STRAIT

24-25 October 1944

Whilst the approach of the Japanese Southern Force had been detected early on the 24th, due to the attacks from the ground-based Japanese aircraft and the fighting in the Sibuyan Sea, only a limited attack was possible on Admiral Nishimura's force as the Japanese ships sailed through the Sulu Sea towards the approaches of the southern entrance to Surigao Strait.

Nishimura's flagship, the battleship *Yamashiro*, experienced numerous near misses from the US aircraft, but she was not significantly damaged. Whilst *Yamashiro* may have escaped comparatively unharmed, *Fusō* suffered far more serious damage, whilst the heavy cruiser *Mogami* and several of the escorting destroyers were damaged by strafing (the destroyer *Shigure* may also have been hit by a bomb). Soon, though, the American attack was over, and the entire force resumed course, heading for the Surigao Strait.

Things, though, seemed to be going well for the Allies at that stage, despite no sightings of the Japanese carriers. The situation, however, was about to change. 'It was evident that the Japanese navy was making a major effort, whether for direct attacks, or transporting troops, or both, was not apparent.' Halsey explained. But, as he later wrote in his despatch, 'If this was to be an all-out attack by the Japanese fleet, there was one piece missing in the puzzle – the carriers.

'They were believed to have been in Japan; and there were sightings which indicated that replenishment measures might have been taken for some important move from Japanese waters. Although our submarines stationed in Japanese water had not reported a carrier force, it was felt they were sure to be employed in some manner in any operation as great as that revealed in the morning of the 24th.'

In the late afternoon of the 24th – at around 15.40 hours – the missing piece was found. Reports reached Halsey of the Japanese Northern Force, with varying numbers of enemy carriers and other ships being claimed.

On the assumption that the weakened Centre Force and the small Southern Force could be easily dealt with by Kincaid's Seventh Fleet and its Support Force, Halsey decided to concentrate all his strength against the Northern Force. This meant that he would not be forming TF 34. He ordered his ships to assemble at a point 150 miles north-east of the San Bernardino Strait to be ready for a dawn attack.

'The night was pregnant with history, wrote one commentator, 'for the coming day was to >>>

Opposite page: A Japanese battleship, either Nishimura's flagship *Yamashiro* or *Fusō*, under attack in the Sulu Sea, 24 October 1944. In the early attacks, about twenty crewmen were killed by strafing and rocket hits on *Yamashiro*. (USNHHC)

seal the fate of an empire. Slowly Admiral Halsey steamed into the night, preceded by planes probing relentlessly for the new antagonist hidden in the northern darkness. Behind him the jaws of the Japanese pincers strained to close the defenceless shipping off the Leyte landings. For in that midnight hour when the American Third Fleet completed its concentration set course for the north, Kurita, braving the hidden dangers of reef and mine, and driving at 20 knots through the San Bernardino Strait was making towards Leyte; while to the south of him, Nishimura, his eyes on the same objective, was approaching the Surigao Strait whose waters were to be his winding sheet.'[7]

Meanwhile, as Halsey raced off to the north, Kincaid, being fully aware of the approaching danger of Nishimura's Southern Force, sent the 7th Fleet Support Force, under the command of Rear Admiral Jesse B. Oldendorf, southwards and its ships were ready and waiting in the Surigao Strait. He had a powerful collection of warships with which to defend the Leyte landings, with six battleships (all but one of which had been damaged or sunk at Pearl Harbor but brought back into service), four heavy and four light cruisers, twenty-eight destroyers and thirty-nine motor torpedo boats. Apart from *Yamashiro* and *Fusō*, Nishimura had just three heavy and one light cruisers, and eleven destroyers immediately under his command.

The first sighting of the Japanese force was made by the radar operator on the patrol boat *PT-131* at 22.15 hours. What had been sighted was probably the cruiser *Mogami* and the Japanese destroyers scouting ahead of the battleships.

Alerted to the approach of the enemy, the MTBs rushed into the attack, firing thirty-four torpedoes at the Japanese ships. Darkness, rain squalls and interference from the enemy's gunfire led to inaccuracy, but seven strikes were claimed. The Japanese opened fire with all their weapons, illuminating the MTBs with searchlights and star shells, and pursuing them with their destroyers.

The next to attack the Southern Force, in the early hours of 25 October, was Captain Jesse Coward's Destroyer Squadron 54. Coward himself, in USS *Remey*, led a division of three on the east side of the strait while his other two ships moved in from the west. Advancing in the darkness, Coward's eastern group of destroyers launched twenty-seven torpedoes just after 03.00 hours. The Japanese opened fire on the eastern destroyers at 03.01 hours, straddling them and forcing them to turn away without firing their guns. The western two destroyers launched twenty torpedoes at about 03.10 hours, the two groups catching the Japanese in a crossfire. The result was devastating.

Two torpedoes from USS *Melvin* struck *Fusō*, inflicting serious damage to the old ship, and she fell out of line. In the noise and confusion of battle, Nishimura did not realise that *Fusō* was no longer behind him.

Then, at 03.20 hours, a torpedo from *Monssen* hit *Yamashiro*, but the battleship was able to continue, though her speed was reduced to 5 knots, with *Mogami* closing up behind her. Two torpedoes from *McDermut* hit the destroyer *Yamagumo*, which blew up with all hands. Another *McDermut* torpedo struck the destroyer *Asagumo*, blowing off her bow and inflicting severe damage that would subsequently prove fatal. At least one more *McDermut* torpedo hit the destroyer *Michishio*, which began to sink.

More agony was then about to be inflicted upon Nishimura's shattered force. Destroyer Squadron 24, under the command of Captain Kenmore M. McManes, began a torpedo attack, from the western flank in two sections, at 03.30 hours. The first section was led by his flagship *Hutchins*, >>>

Opposite page: Japanese capital ships under attack on 24 October. Again, this could be either of the battleships *Yamashiro* or *Fusō* under fire, along with the cruiser *Mogami*. (USNHHC)

the second section by HMAS *Arunta*. The explosion of *Yamagumo*, caused by *McDermut*'s torpedo, lit the scene, exposing the Japanese warships. The destroyer *Shigure* dodged four torpedoes from *Arunta*. One torpedo from USS *Killen* struck *Yamashiro* (her second torpedo hit), causing Nishimura to issue a 'general attack' order – in other words all ships attack independently. More torpedoes then slammed into the stricken *Michishio*, hastening her demise.

The remorseless assault upon the Japanese Southern Force continued, the next attack being delivered by Captain Roland Smoot's Destroyer Squadron 56. The squadron attacked in three sections. By this time, *Yamashiro* had shaken off the second torpedo hit and resumed her forward advance with the so-far undamaged *Mogami*. But *Fusō* suffered yet another torpedo strike, broke up, or exploded, and sank. A huge underwater explosion ignited a large pool of the highly volatile fuel in which *Fusō* survivors were swimming. Only about ten of her crew of 1,600 survived, many dying horribly in the burning fuel.

As she struggled on through the Strait, *Yamashiro* reached the narrows where Oldendorf had assembled his main line of battleships. Behind a screen of cruisers, which included HMAS *Shropshire*, the six battleships of his force trained their guns toward the approaching enemy. >>>

Opposite page: Rear Admiral Jesse B. Oldendorf, commander of the 7th Fleet Support Force. His actions on 24 and 25 October 1944 prevented the Japanese from bringing their battle fleet into Surigao Strait and attacking the beachheads on Leyte Island.

Below: A view of the battleships *Fusō* (background) and *Yamashiro* (foreground), with the battleship *Haruna* in the distant background, at anchor before the events of October 1944. During the American aerial attacks on 24 October, a direct bomb hit beside *Fusō*'s No.2 twin 14-inch gun turret and sprang leaks in the hull that could not be closed and seawater had to continuously be pumped out for the remainder of the subsequent battle. Another bomb hit the quarterdeck, destroying both of *Fusō*'s floatplanes and starting an aviation gasoline fire, that as it turned out looked worse than it was. (National Museum of the US Navy)

After Oldendorf's cruisers engaged the enemy at 03.51 hours, his battleships' 16-inch guns roared to life two minutes later. Smoot watched the massive broadside from the American battleships: 'The devastating accuracy of this gunfire was the most beautiful sight I have ever witnessed. The arched line of tracers in the darkness looked like a continual stream of lighted railroad cars going over a hill. No target could be observed at first, then shortly there would be fires and explosions, and another enemy ship would be accounted for.'[8]

The rear column of the Southern Force, the Second Striking Force, commanded by Vice Admiral Shima, then appeared in the Strait, with the light cruiser *Abukuma* being hit by a torpedo fired from a motor torpedo boat. Seeing the remnants of Nishimura's force withdrawing, Shima also turned around, but in the ensuing confusion his flagship *Nachi* collided with *Mogami*. Both were badly damaged and later *Mogami* was abandoned before being sunk after she was shelled by the advancing US cruisers and struck by naval torpedo-bombers.

Only one of Nishimura's seven ships, *Shigure*, escaped. With its departure, the threat from the Southern Force was well and truly eliminated.

Below: US Navy motor torpedo boats preparing for their part in the Battle of Surigao Strait, on or around 24 October 1944. In the foreground is USS *PT-131*. The image was taken from the decks of USS *Wachapreague*, a motor torpedo boat tender. Note the Mark XIII torpedoes, rockets, mortar (on top of *PT-131*'s forward deckhouse), 20mm cannon and .50 calibre machine-guns carried by these PT boats. (NARA)

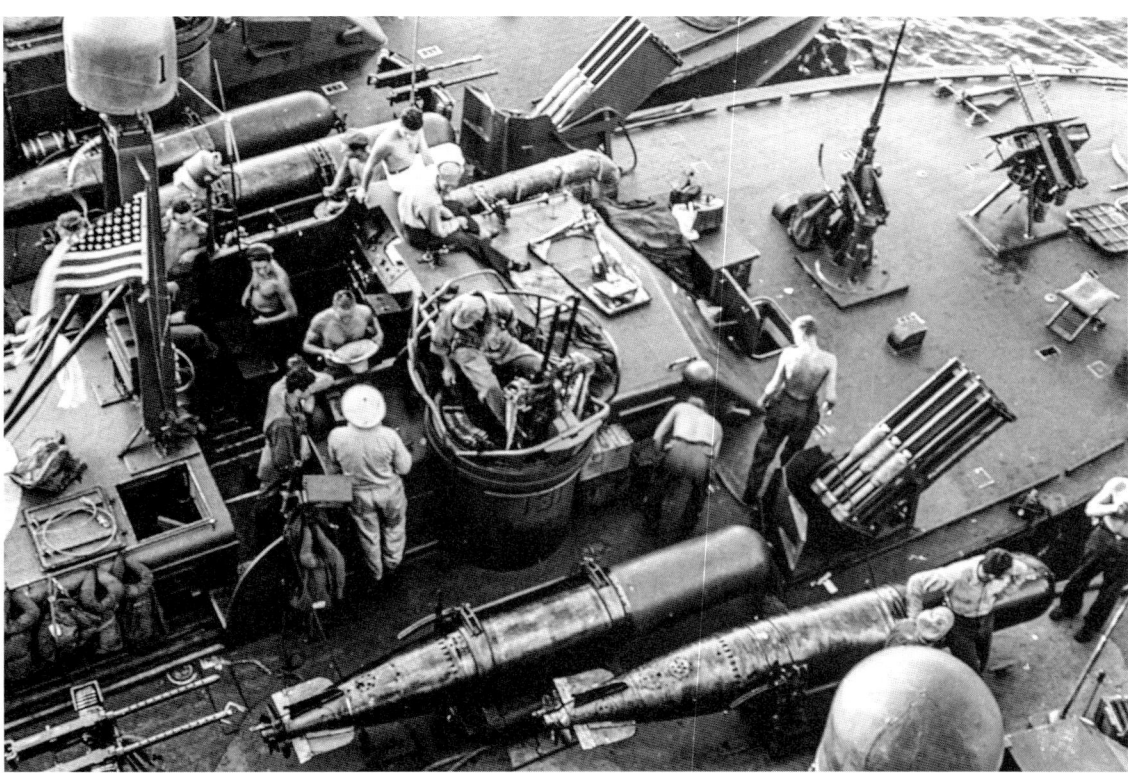

Above: A watercolour by Commander Dwight Shepler of an MTB manoeuvring at speed in what he called 'Action in Surigao Strait'. (USNHHC)

Below: Damage to *PT-152* which was caused by an enemy shell during the battle. Though the MTBs probably caused little damage to the enemy, the attack by these small craft, of which only one was sunk, must have thrown the Southern Force off balance and certainly contributed to Nishimura's eventual defeat. (USNHHC)

BATTLE OF LEYTE GULF

Right: The USS *Melvin*, which was known to its crew as the 'Merciless Melvin', underway. An officer on the cruiser *Mogami*, steaming in formation behind *Yamashiro* and described the result of the destroyer's attack: 'Direct torpedo hit [observed] on starboard side of amidships, causing ship to list to starboard and lose speed fell back, and *Mogami* moved on behind *Yamashiro*. Thereafter several torpedo attacks received, interspersed with intermittent and accurate enemy shellfire.'[9] (USNHHC)

Below: For his actions during the battle, Captain Roland Smoot, shown here as a Rear Admiral, was awarded the first of his two Navy Crosses, the citation for which read: 'Leading his ships in a daring and successful attack on the enemy battle-line, by his courage, skill in combat, and determination, Commodore Smoot gave encouragement to his force in a manner that caused his action to be very instrumental in the success of this most difficult operation.' (USNHHC)

Above: As she struggled on through the Strait, *Yamashiro* reached the narrows where Oldendorf had assembled his main line of battle ships. Behind a screen of cruisers, which included HMAS *Shropshire*, the six battleships of his force trained their guns toward the approaching enemy. Here flashes from the guns of the cruisers can be seen as they engage the Japanese force, as photographed from the battleship USS *Pennsylvania*. (NARA)

Right: Positioned at the northern exit of the Surigao Strait, the gunners on the cruiser USS *Portland* opened fire on the approaching *Mogami* at 04.00 hours on the 25th. For his part in the action, *Portland*'s captain, Captain Thomas G.W. Settle, was awarded the Navy Cross – seen here being bestowed by Vice Admiral Oldendorf. (National Museum of the US Navy)

Opposite page: To the mighty 14- and 16-inch salvos of the battleships and the 8-inch broadsides of the heavy cruisers was added the incessant barrage of the light cruisers, such as USS *Phoenix*, shown here, which could fire 200 or more 6-inch rounds per minute. (USNHHC)

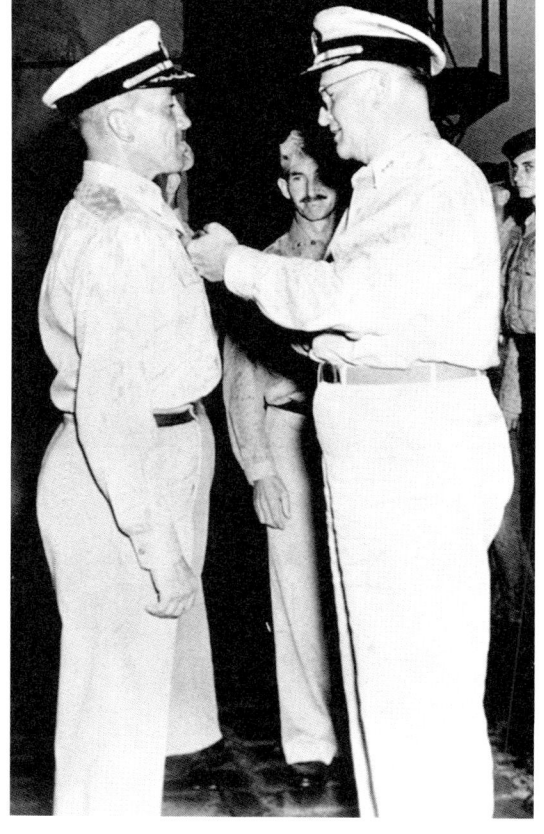

BATTLES OF THE SULU SEA AND THE SURIGAO STRAIT

BATTLE OF LEYTE GULF

BATTLES OF THE SULU SEA AND THE SURIGAO STRAIT

Opposite page top: A scene on board the battleship USS *Pennsylvania*, more specifically the sky control, during the battle. *Pennsylvania* had some trouble locating a target in the darkness of the early hours of the 25th, her older Mk.3 radar not being as effective as the more modern sets on *West Virginia* and some of the other battleships. (USNHHC)

Opposite page bottom: USS *West Virginia* lights up the night sky as she unleashes a salvo during the early hours of the 25th. Oldendorf gave the order to open fire at 03.51 hours, *West Virginia* doing so first one minute later, followed by *Tennessee* and *California*, all three concentrating their fire on *Yamashiro*. (USNHHC)

Below: US Navy battleships pictured off Battleships off Leyte, 20-24 October 1944. They are, left to right, USS *Mississippi*, USS *West Virginia*, and USS *Maryland*. The duel of the battleships in the Surigao Strait lasted just ten minutes, with *Mississippi* firing the last salvo. This was the last salvo ever fired by a battleship against another battleship in history. Shells smashed into *Yamashiro* and *Mogami*. A torpedo from the destroyer USS *Bennion* finished off *Yamashiro*. (USNHHC)

Main image: Native and US military craft pictured searching for Japanese survivors during rescue operations in the Surigao Strait, October 1944. (USNHHC)

BATTLES OF THE SULU SEA AND THE SURIGAO STRAIT

Left: Members of the crew of *PT-321* haul a Japanese survivor out of the waters of the Surigao Strait, October 1944. Note the head of a second individual who can be seen in the water by the first man's feet. (National Museum of the US Navy)

Above: The 'kills' scoreboard on the side of the fire control tower of USS *Melvin* pictured later in the war in 1945. At the top, on the left, is the symbol denoting the battleship *Fusō*. (USNHHC)

Above: Filipinos come out to assist the US Navy PT Boats in picking up Japanese survivors after the engagement in the Surigao Strait. (National Museum of the US Navy)

Below: Captain Kenmore M. McManes describes the events of the Battle of Surigao Strait to Secretary of the Navy James Forrestal (standing, with pipe) and others in Washington D.C., December 1944. For his actions as commander of Destroyer Squadron 24 on the night of 24-25 October 1944, McManes was awarded the Navy Cross. (US Navy)

Chapter 5

THE BATTLE OFF SAMAR

25 October 1944

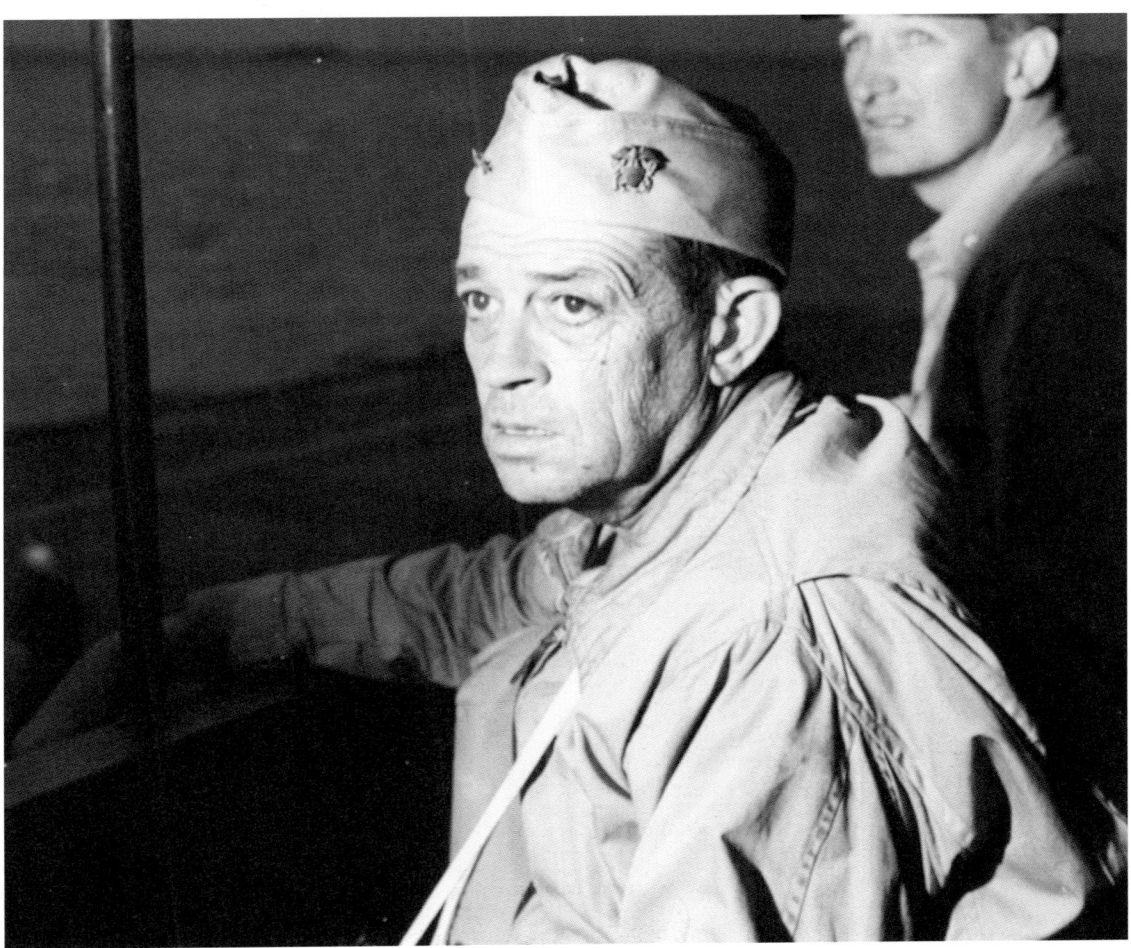

Above: With its official title of Task Unit 77.4.3, Rear Admiral Clifton 'Ziggy' Sprague's *Taffy* 3 comprised two light carrier divisions with a protective screen of seven destroyers and destroyer escorts. In Carrier Division 25 were USS *Fanshaw Bay*, *St. Lo*, *White Plains*, *Kalinin Bay*, whilst in Rear Admiral Ralph A. Ofstie's Carrier Division 26 were *Kitkun Bay* and *Gambier Bay*. Proving screening for *Taffy* 3 were the destroyers *Hoel*, *Heermann* and *Johnston*, and destroyer escorts *Dennis*, *John C. Butler*, *Raymond*, and *Samuel B. Roberts*. Clifton Sprague is shown here on *Fanshaw Bay*. (USNHHC)

BATTLE OF LEYTE GULF

Since the never-to-be-forgotten attack on the US Pacific Fleet's base at Pearl Harbor, it had been the Japanese aircraft carriers which had been at the forefront of Japanese operations and had caused the American admirals the most anxiety. Though the Japanese had suffered terrible losses in both aircraft and carriers during the intervening three years, it was the air arm of the Imperial Japanese Navy which was considered its most lethal weapon. 'If we destroyed those carriers,' Halsey wrote, 'future operations need fear no major threat from the sea.' Halsey, therefore, gathered together every available ship of the Third Fleet and headed north to face Ozawa's Northern Force. 'We had chosen our antagonist, continued Halsey. 'It remained only to choose the best way to meet him.'

At around 19.50 hours on the evening of 24 October, Halsey relayed his decision to Kincaid and his Seventh Fleet: 'Central Force heavily damaged according to strike reports. Am proceeding north with three groups to attack [enemy] carrier force at dawn.' Off Halsey went with the whole of the Third Fleet. So, with the 7th Fleet Support Force engaging the Japanese Southern Force, and the

Below: At 06.37 hours on the 25th, Ensign William C. Brooks, flying a TBF Avenger from the carrier *St. Lo* sighted a naval force which, though he had expected to be from Halsey's Third Fleet, in fact appeared to be Japanese. This information was immediately fed back to Admiral Sprague, who, taken aback by the news, requested positive identification. Brooks duly replied, 'I see the biggest meatball flag on the biggest battleship I ever saw!' He had located the largest of the three attacking enemy forces, which consisted of four battleships, including Kurita's flagship *Yamato*, which alone displaced as much as all units of *Taffy 3* combined, six heavy cruisers, two light cruisers and some ten destroyers. Here *Yamato*, with a cruiser, either *Tone* or *Chikuma*, on her port quarter, has been photographed underway off Samar, by an aircraft from USS *Petrof Bay*, on 25 October. (US Navy)

Above: A few minutes after the initial contact, the Japanese force came into view. Almost immediately, Sprague ordered his ships to make smoke while the carriers turned into the wind and launched their aircraft. Taken from USS *Kalanin Bay*, this photograph shows the USS *Gambier Bay* and two destroyer escorts making smoke. At the point it was taken, notes the original caption, Japanese warships were 'faintly visible on the horizon'. (USNHHC)

Third Fleet steaming towards the Japanese Northern Force, the San Bernadino Strait was unguarded.

Vice Admiral Takeo Kurita's Centre Force duly passed through it unchallenged. Ahead, however, were the three carrier groups of the Seventh Fleet, call-signs *Taffy 1, 2* and *3* respectively, with their destroyer escorts. In theory they stood little chance against Kurita's battleships and cruisers.

It was *Taffy 3*, the most northerly group and the closest to the San Bernardino Strait, which first sighted the approaching Japanese warships on 25 October. Almost immediately, Rear Admiral Clifton Sprague ordered his ships to make smoke while his carriers turned into the wind and launched all their aircraft, irrespective of their state of readiness. While they were doing this, the guns of the Japanese ships roared. Sprague later reflected that, 'It did not appear any of our ships could survive another five minutes.'

But rather than run, the carriers' escorting destroyers attacked. The Japanese cruiser *Kumano* was hit and set on fire. The destroyers charged towards the Japanese ships with suicidal bravery.

BATTLE OF LEYTE GULF

Three of them were sunk, as was the carrier USS *Gambier Bay*. But their attacks, and those from the aircraft of *Taffy 2*, were so relentless that Kurita, after losing another two cruisers, gave up the struggle and retreated.

Sprague later admitted that he could not believe his eyes when he saw the Japanese ships turn back. Rear Admiral Samuel Eliot Morison concluded that, 'In no engagement in its entire history has the United States Navy shown more gallantry, guts and gumption than in the two morning hours … off Samar.'

Opposite: The Japanese Centre Force was led by the battleships *Yamato*, *Nagato*, *Kongo* and *Haruna* in the centre of the battle line. On the right flank were the heavy cruisers *Chokai* and *Haguro* and on the left, the heavy cruisers *Kumano*, *Suzuya*, *Chikuma* and *Tone*. Two destroyer flotillas were posted on the port and starboard bows. The battleships opened fire almost as soon as the American ships were spotted, *Yamato* firing first at a distance of 35,000 yards. For the first time, the 3,220lb shells of the super-battleship were propelled at an enemy surface target from the 70-foot-long barrels of its monstrous guns. Here USS *Kitkun Bay* prepares to launch its FM-2 Wildcat fighters while, in the distance, shells are splashing near the escort carrier USS *White Plains*. (USNHHC)

Below: The enormous enemy shells began splashing around Sprague's comparatively small ships. Tremendous splashes, vibrantly coloured by dye, sprouted along the wakes of the American vessels. 'When they hit, they had dye in them. Another would be green or blue, or whatever they were, and they could see where they missed and correct for it,' recalled Electrician's Mate Orville Bethard. 'Our captain got kinda smart about that and if any of them got close to us, instead of running from it, he would go right into where they just shot and they were correcting and missing us because of that.'[10] This image shows US destroyers and other escorts laying a smoke screen, while under fire (note the splashes from the Japanese shells) on 25 October 1944. (US National Naval Aviation Museum)

Below: At 07.05 hours, Sprague broadcast a contact report and asked for assistance. Kincaid responded by ordering all available surface forces to concentrate at the eastern end of Leyte Gulf, preparatory to moving up to support the escort carriers. He also messaged Halsey asking for help. All aircraft were recalled from support missions and sent to attack Kurita's fast approaching force. *Taffy 2*'s Felix Stump replied to Sprague's appeal: 'Don't be alarmed. Remember we're back of you. Don't get excited! Don't do anything rash!'[11] A portrait of Admiral Felix B. Stump taken after the war. (USNHHC)

Right: With the firepower he had available, Kurita should have ploughed straight into Sprague's formation and blown *Taffy 3* to bits. Instead, the Japanese commander tried to encircle the US ships. Sprague continued to manoeuvre with all his ships making so much smoke, both funnel and chemical, that Kurita and his men were continually off-balanced. USS *Heermann* is shown here laying smoke early in the battle. (USNHHC)

BATTLE OF LEYTE GULF

Main image: Another view of *Heermann* and another escort making extremely black smoke which helped conceal the exact positions of the constantly moving ships of *Taffy 3*. It might have been thought that Sprague would have wanted to continue to manoeuvre and keep as far away from the Japanese as possible. But the slow-moving escort carriers could never hope to outrun the fast enemy battleships. There was only one alternative to running away, and that was staying to fight. At 07.16 hours, Sprague ordered his destroyers to carry out torpedo attacks. With *Johnston* in the lead, followed by *Heermann*, and *Hoel*, the three destroyers turned and raced towards Kurita's huge warships. (USNHHC)

THE BATTLE OFF SAMAR

BATTLE OF LEYTE GULF

Main image: *Johnston* managed to damage the heavy cruiser *Kumano* with a torpedo strike which cut off part of her bow, but was in turn heavily damaged by 6- and 14-inch shells. *Hoel* fired at, and missed, the battleship *Kongo*, and was also hit multiple times. For a while, she was boxed in by Japanese battleships and cruisers, all of which fired at her. *Heermann* then entered the fray launching torpedoes at the Japanese heavy cruiser *Haguru*, but *Haguru* evaded the torpedoes and fired multiple salvos at the destroyer, which all missed. Moving beyond the Japanese cruiser division, *Heermann* came upon the battleships *Kongo*, *Yamato*, and *Nagato*, firing her remaining torpedoes and 5-inch guns at *Kongo*. The destroyer then quickly came about and moved to a screening station on the starboard flank of the carriers. Despite the intensity of Japanese fire, the only damage aboard *Heermann* had been caused by shell fragments. The strike suffered by *Kumano* caused its speed to be reduced to 16 knots and Vice Admiral Shiraisha transferred his flag to the heavy cruiser *Suzuya*, which for a time stood by her. USS *Johnston* (DD-557) seen here off Seattle or Tacoma, Washington, almost exactly a year earlier, 27 October 1943. (USNHHC)

THE BATTLE OFF SAMAR

BATTLE OF LEYTE GULF

Below: Throughout this period the Japanese ships had come under almost continuous assault from the aircraft of Taffy 3 as well as Taffy 2. Just after the Japanese force had been sighted by Taffy 3, Admiral Stump had his available TBM Avengers re-armed with torpedoes or 500-pound bombs capable of damaging capital ships. As Taffy 3 was being pursued, Stump closed the distance to Sprague's task unit and was able to launch three strikes during the battle. 'Things really got popping,' recalled Zachery Z. Zink on board Taffy 2's USS Kadashan Bay. 'All planes got armed with torpedoes, bombs and everything we had. We only had 7 torpedoes; they were the first to go. We were not supposed to be in a situation like this.'[12] This image shows Yamato under attack as an Avenger from Kadashan Bay approaches the great battleship. (USNHHC)

Right: A Japanese destroyer firing at the aircraft from Taffy 3 as photographed by one of USS White Plains' aircraft. (USNHHC)

BATTLE OF LEYTE GULF

Opposite page top: By 07.38 hours on the 25th, the foremost cruiser was no more than 14,000 yards behind the carrier *St. Lo*, while another cruiser and what appeared to be a large destroyer moved up to within 12,000 yards of the task unit and delivered repeated full broadsides at the American ships. *St. Lo*'s Action Report noted that there were 'flashes from all six of the cruiser's turrets as salvos were fired'. None of the Japanese cruisers had six turrets, but the huge Japanese cruisers, the largest afloat, were so powerfully armed that their salvos must have given the impression of being even greater than they were. Nevertheless, up to this point none of the American ships had been hit by the Japanese. Here we see Japanese shells falling short of USS *Kalinin Bay*; smoke from the enemy warships can just be seen in the distance. (USNHHC)

Opposite page bottom: The scene on the flight deck of USS *Kalinin Bay* as she is near-missed by Japanese shells. It has been estimated that the Japanese fired 300 salvos before they hit any of the American ships. (US Navy)

Below: Kurita had not assigned his captains any specific targets, each being permitted to take advantage of whatever situation presented itself. But the Japanese rate of fire was very slow, being more than a minute between salvos, which gave even the clumsy and slow American escort carriers time to manoeuvre. The carriers had also been told at 07.40 hours by Sprague to open fire with their own single 5-inch guns as soon as the enemy ships were within their 14,000-yard range. *Gambier Bay* and *St. Lo* opened fire immediately, with the others joining in as soon as they were able. Though a number of hits were claimed, the 55lb shells had little effect against the thick armour of the enemy cruisers. During this period, *White Plains* and *Fanshaw Bay* in particular, were under sustained gunfire yet still emerged unscathed – it was from the former that these splashes from Japanese shells were photographed. (USNHHC)

BATTLE OF LEYTE GULF

Right: Also, at 07.40 hours, Sprague ordered his destroyers to make a second torpedo attack. *Johnston* attacked first, firing a full salvo at one of the heavy cruisers. She received heavy damage but continued to fire her guns at ranges down to 5,000 yards. In the fighting *Johnston*'s captain, Lieutenant Commander Ernest E. Evans, was wounded but, as the citation for his award of the Navy Cross makes clear, this did not stop him for a moment:

'The first to lay a smokescreen and to open fire as an enemy task force, vastly superior in number, firepower and armor, rapidly approached. Comdr. Evans gallantly diverted the powerful blasts of hostile guns from the lightly armed and armored carriers under his protection, launching the first torpedo attack when the *Johnston* came under straddling Japanese shellfire.

'Undaunted by damage sustained under the terrific volume of fire, he unhesitatingly joined others of his group to provide fire support during subsequent torpedo attacks against the Japanese and, outshooting and out-manoeuvring the enemy as he consistently interposed his vessel between the hostile fleet units and our carriers despite the crippling loss of engine power and communications with steering aft, shifted command to the fantail, shouted steering orders through an open hatch to men turning the rudder by hand and battled furiously until the *Johnston*, burning and shuddering from a mortal blow, lay dead in the water after 3 hours of fierce combat. Seriously wounded early in the engagement, Comdr. Evans, by his indomitable courage and brilliant professional skill, aided materially in turning back the enemy during a critical phase of the action.' At 10.10 hours *Johnston* rolled over and sank.

Though accounts regarding is fate vary, it was reported that Evans was last seen alive, wounded, and wearing a life jacket, in the water with other survivors on the night of 25 October. One survivor recalled other officers with him clinging to 4x4-inch timbers, shoring that had evidently drifted off the ship when she sank.

Lieutenant Commander Evans is pictured here at the commissioning ceremony of USS *Johnston* at Seattle on 27 October 1943. (USNHHC)

Main image: *Hoel* was next, launching a half-salvo at one of the battleships at a range of 9,000 yards. Almost immediately, she was hit, and her port engine and steering engine were out of action but, steering by hand, *Hoel* continued to fire her guns at the battleships and cruisers which were then either side of her. A few minutes later, *Hoel* fired another half-salvo of torpedoes, striking one of the cruisers at 4,000 yards. But the crew had no time to observe the results of their torpedoes as *Hoel* came under another barrage of shells. Her No.3 gun was unusable because of steam escaping from the engine room, the barrel of No.4 gun was shot off by a direct hit and a very near miss rendered No.5 gun inoperable. The only reason she stayed afloat was because the Japanese were using armour-piercing shells that for the most part passed through the thin plates of her hull without exploding. But the destroyer was struck again and again and, riddled by some forty holes from 5-inch, 8-inch and 14-inch shells, was clearly in serious trouble. At 08.55 hours *Hoel* sank while her crew were trying desperately to repair the battle damage. This view of *Hoel* is dated 3 August 1944. (NARA)

BATTLE OF LEYTE GULF

Main image: *Heermann* was more fortunate. While no results were observed from her first salvo of torpedoes fired at 07.54 hours, six minutes later she fired a further three torpedoes at one of the huge battleships and was able to claim one hit. *Heermann* survived the battle and the war, with this photograph of her being dated December 1959. (USNHHC)

THE BATTLE OFF SAMAR

Above: According to the action report of *Samuel B. Roberts*, 'The crew were informed over the loud speaker system at the beginning of the action, of the Commanding Officer's estimate of the situation, that is, a fight against overwhelming odds from which survival could not be expected, during which time we would do what damage we could. In the face of this knowledge the men zealously manned their stations wherever they might be, and fought and worked with such calmness, courage and efficiency that no higher honor could be conceived than to command such a group of men.' Under cover of the swirling smoke, the destroyer approached a heavy cruiser to within 4,000 yards before releasing her torpedoes at about 08.00 hours. She was untouched up to that point. *Samuel B. Roberts* is seen here in October 1944, just a week or two before the battle. (Courtesy of the USS Samuel B. Roberts Survivors Association)

Right: But *Samuel B. Roberts'* luck was about to run out. Three 8-inch rounds struck her on the port side. Though none exploded, passing right through the ship, two of them exited below the waterline, and water began to pour into the forward ammunition handling room and the compartment housing the ship's master gyro, shorting out all the electrical power to the radios, radar and gun mounts. The third round caused even more damage, cutting right through her main steam line in the forward fire room. Losing speed and manoeuvrability, *Samuel B. Roberts* was an easy target. Almost immediately four more rounds smashed into the stricken escort destroyer. Clearly sinking and unable to fire her weapons, Lieutenant Commander Robert W. Copeland ordered the crew to abandon ship. After the last of his men had cleared the ship, Copeland also left, pausing momentarily to see his ship for the last time: 'I could look from the deck up through the bottom of the boat. It was a sight I will never forget. That one picture summed up the whole desolate destruction of a living ship with living men coming into the emptiness of nothing. I realised that I was the only person alive on that side of the ship. A feeling of loneliness came over me. It made me shudder … Down on the deck there lay three men, two of whom I could identify and one I couldn't. They were dead.'[13] Commander Copeland received the Navy Cross for his heroism in command of *Samuel B. Roberts* on 16 July 1945 from Rear Admiral David M. LeBreton. (USNHHC)

Below: Astonishingly, it was not until 07.50 hours that the Japanese ships managed to hit any of the escort carriers, when an 8-inch shell struck *Fanshaw Bay*'s bow, damaging its catapult. But, gradually, the Japanese cruisers and destroyers were able to close on *Gambier Bay* and *Kalinin Bay* on the north-western flank of the task unit. *Kalinin Bay* was hit three or four times but without suffering any critical damage. That was not the case, though, with *Gambier Bay*. Despite coming under heavy fire she had managed to remain undamaged by constant changes of direction, but at 08.10 she received her first hit. From that time onwards, she was struck time and time again suffering at least fifteen hits. Here *Gambier Bay* is bracketed by Japanese shells while making smoke. After these near misses, the carrier appeared to slow down and fall behind the rest of her task group. (National Museum of the US Navy)

BATTLE OF LEYTE GULF

Opposite page: The most telling hits on *Gambier Bay* punctured boilers, opened a hole in the forward engine room that began heavy flooding, and destroyed the steering. At 08.40 a shell entered number three boiler in the after engine room, all steam pressure was lost and at 08.45 the ship was dead in the water, devoid of all power, and sinking with three Japanese cruisers still hammering at her from point blank range. The ship was listing badly to port as the crew prepared to abandon ship. There was utter confusion, men running all around, some terribly wounded. *Gambier Bay* seen here, through the smokescreen, under heavy fire and already falling behind the other escort carriers. (USNHHC)

Below: Members of the crew of USS *Kitkun Bay* can only watch as *Gambier Bay* falls even further behind the rest of her task group on 25 October. (National Museum of the US Navy)

BATTLE OF LEYTE GULF

Opposite page top: A painting by C.G. Evers depicting *Gambier Bay*'s final hour. *Gambier Bay* was the only American aircraft carrier sunk by enemy surface gunfire during the Second World War. (United States Naval Institute)

Opposite page bottom: At approximately 08.30 hours five Japanese destroyers bore down on *Kalinin Bay*. The destroyers fired upon the escort carrier which replied with its single 5-inch gun. Once more, the Japanese failed to hit their target, yet *Kalinin Bay* was able to claim a strike on one of the destroyers causing it to become enveloped in white smoke. *Taffy 3*'s escorts moved to help, and to some extent drew the Japanese destroyers away. At 08.36 hours, two Japanese cruisers emerged from the smoke and Sprague ordered *Dennis* and *Raymond* to intervene and try to cover the carriers with smoke yet again and to try and distract the cruisers. In these efforts *Dennis* reported a hit below the waterline and that her main battery was out of action. As for *Raymond*, she had no smoke or torpedoes left but she still charged towards the cruisers. Incredibly, though shells fell all around, she was not hit, and her aggressive advance compelled the cruisers to turn away. This watercolour by Commander Dwight Shepler depicts the counterattack by the escort carrier group's screen. (USNHHC)

Below: Before the Japanese cruisers turned away, they had managed to score ten strikes on *Kalinin Bay* to add to the earlier hits she had sustained. The escort carrier remained afloat, once again due to the fact that the Japanese ships fired armour-piercing and not high explosive shells. This is a view of some of the damage to *Kalinin Bay*'s flight deck after one of the two kamikaze attacks she endured on 25 October. (US National Naval Aviation Museum)

BATTLE OF LEYTE GULF

THE BATTLE OFF SAMAR

Main image: *Kalinin Bay* is seen in this photograph arriving at San Diego, California on 25 November 1944 for repairs to the damage. (USNHHC)

BATTLE OF LEYTE GULF

Above: Rear Admiral Thomas L. Sprague (no relation to Clifton Sprague) in command of *Taffy 1* was about 120 miles to the south of the battle that raged around *Taffy 3*, and upon receiving his namesake's call for help, he sent all his aircraft into the fray. In this photograph we can see a Japanese Tone-class cruiser taken by a plane from *Taffy 1*'s USS *Petrof Bay*. (USNHHC)

Below: However, quite unexpectedly a Japanese aircraft appeared on the scene. The raider flew straight into the escort carrier USS *Santee*, crashing through the flight deck into the hangar below. A little while later, at 07.53 hours, *Santee* was hit again, this time by a torpedo, a photographer on USS *Petrof Bay* managed to capture the moment that the torpedo struck. (NARA)

Above: Six minutes later, another suicide aircraft crashed into another of *Taffy 1*'s escort carriers, USS *Suwannee*.

This is one of a sequence of shots taken from USS *Petrof Bay* which reveal the Japanese Mitsubishi A6M 'Zero' kamikaze aircraft approaching and then crashing into *Suwannee*. (National Museum of the US Navy)

Below: Pictured from USS *Sangamon*, a plume of smoke and debris rises into the air following the kamikaze's impact with the flight deck of USS *Suwannee*. The aircraft that can be seen over the carrier is a defending US fighter. (National Museum of the US Navy)

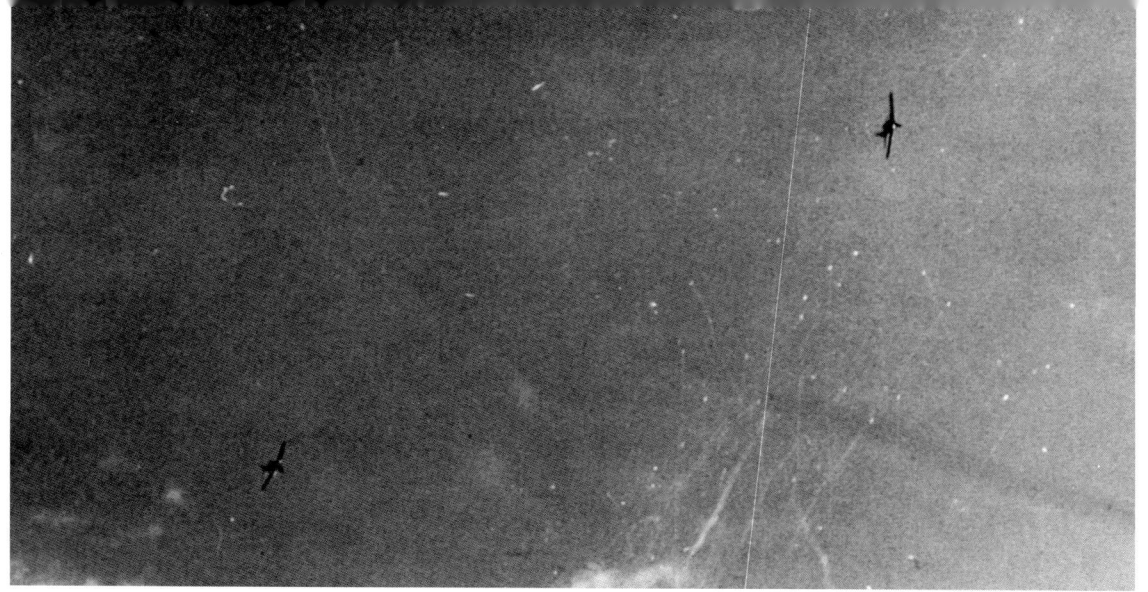

THE BATTLE OFF SAMAR

Opposite page top: The Grumman F6F Hellcat of Ensign Paul W. Lindskog, of VF 60, attempts to intercept the kamikaze, despite increasing anti-aircraft from the guns on USS *Suwannee*. A few seconds later the Mitsubishi A6M slammed into the carrier just forward of the after elevator 1944. (USNHHC)

Opposite page bottom: Taken from USS *Petrof Bay*, this photograph shows an F6F Hellcat, presumably that of Ensign Lindskog, banking away after chasing the kamikaze which had just crashed into USS *Suwannee*. (USNHHC)

Below: The Mitsubishi A6M struck USS *Suwannee* about 40 feet forward of the carrier's after elevator, tearing a large hole in the flight deck.

The kamikaze's bomb compounded the fracture when it exploded between the flight and hangar decks, which caused the smoke that can be seen here billowing out. (National Museum of the US Navy)

Above: The hole in the flight deck of USS *Suwannee* following the kamikaze attack. Lieutenant Walter B. Burwell was the Medical Officer onboard. Along with one of his corpsmen, he tried to reach men trapped on the forecastle by the fire that broke out. Taking first aid bags with morphine and bandages, Burwell grabbed a fire extinguisher and, dodging the flames, the two men made their way forward: 'We managed to work our way up several decks, through passageways along the wrecked and burning combat information center and decoding area, through officers' country, and finally out on the forecastle. Many of the crew on the forecastle and the catwalks above it had been blown over the side by the explosions. But others trapped below and aft of the forecastle area found themselves under a curtain of fire from aviation gasoline pouring down from burning planes on the flight deck above.

Their only escape was to leap aflame into the sea, but some were trapped so that they were incinerated before they could leap. By the time we arrived on the forecastle, the flow of gasoline had

THE BATTLE OFF SAMAR

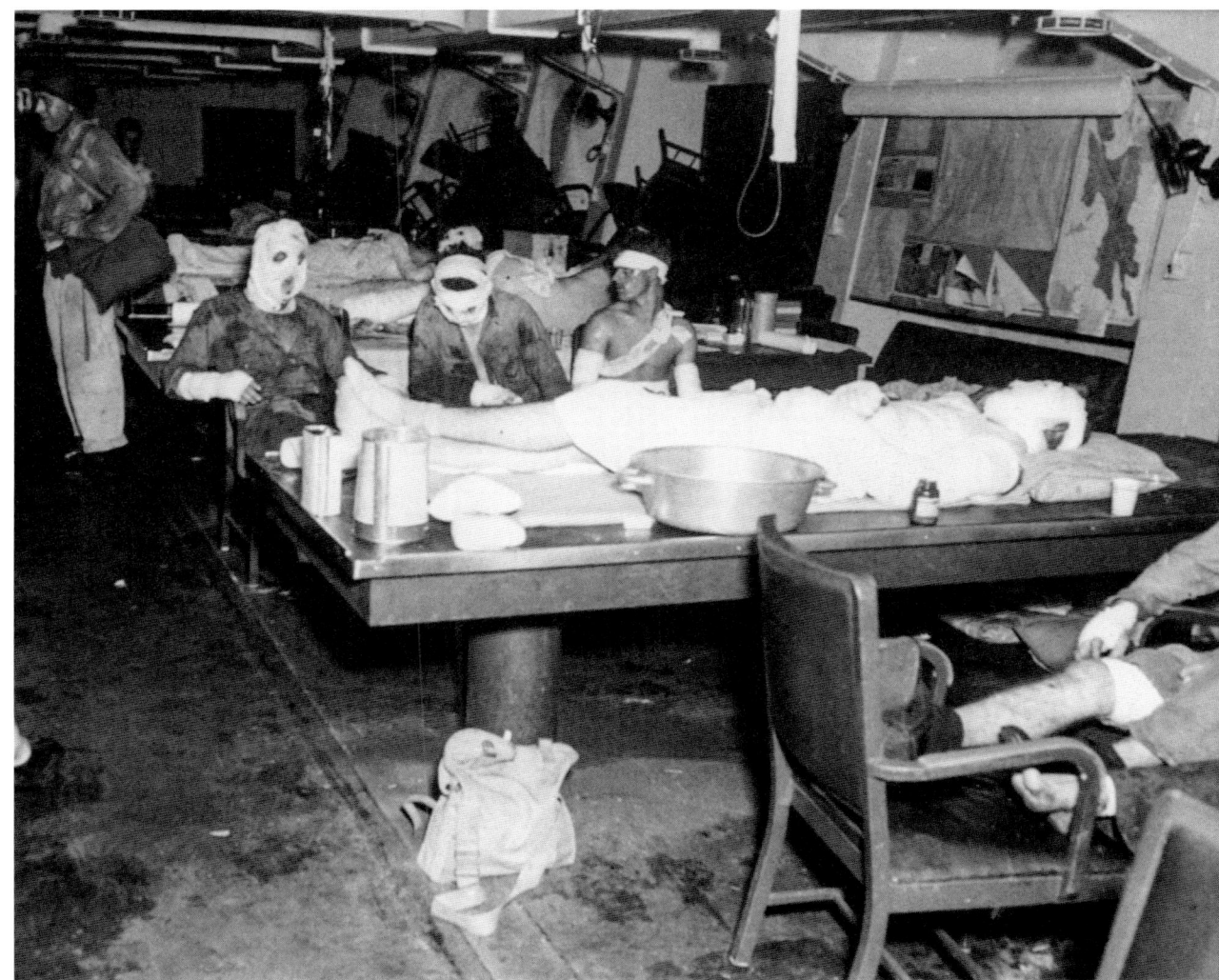

mostly consumed itself, and flames were only erupting and flickering from combustible areas of water and oil. Nonetheless, the decks and bulkheads were still blistering hot and ammunition in the small arms locker on the deck below was popping from the heat like strings of firecrackers. With each salvo of popping, two or three more panicky crew men would leap over the side, and we found that our most urgent task was to persuade those poised on the rail not to jump by a combination of physical restraint and reassurance that fires were being controlled and that more help was on the way. Most of the remaining wounded in the forecastle area were severely burned beyond recognition and hope.'[14] (National Museum of the US Navy)

Above: USS *Suwannee*'s wardroom in use as an emergency sick bay to help the burned and wounded men. The carrier endured further kamikaze attacks during the hours that followed. *Suwannee*'s casualties for 25–26 October were 107 dead and 160 wounded. (USNHHC)

Above: The Japanese ships themselves came under attack from *Taffy 3*'s aircraft, including that of Ensign Paul Bennett, who, in his TBM torpedo bomber, was possibly the last pilot to fly off *Gambier Bay* before she sank. Unable to land on *Gambier Bay* he flew on to *Taffy 2*, landing on USS *Manila Bay* from where he joined in *Taffy 2*'s attack on the Centre Force: 'We were refuelled, loaded with 4x500 lb bombs, and headed back north. Since I was not part of their squadron, I was tail end charley in the strike. We attacked a Japanese cruiser but the planes in front of me were missing the target with their bombs, because we were instructed to set our bomb releases for an interval so they would drop one at a time.

When the plane ahead of me started his dive, I waited to get an interval so we did not collide over the target. As I started in, I saw the splashes from his bombs, straddling the cruiser as it was turning. By this time I was in my dive, and I pulled the bomb release and the first bomb dropped. I saw that I

would be about abeam when the bombs got to the target, so that my chances of a hit were almost nil. I then pulled the emergency bomb release and dumped all 3 remaining bombs at once on what we have assumed was the Japanese cruiser *Suzuya*. Although I couldn't see it, my radioman and gunner both confirmed the hit. I then went south again and landed on the *Fanshaw Bay*, which was on its way out of the battle area.'[15] Paul Bennett's Avenger was one of six of *Taffy 3*'s aircraft that landed on *Taffy 2*'s carriers, others landed at Tacloban airfield on Leyte. *Suzuya*, shown here, was part of Kurita's Cruiser Division 7. (USNHHC)

Above: The first strike by *Taffy 2*'s aircraft had reportedly hit two heavy and one light enemy cruisers. The second strike claimed two torpedo hits on a heavy cruiser and one on a battleship. Here a Tone-class cruiser is firing at attacking aircraft. (USNHHC)

Above: The claims of the American flyers were not exaggerated. The heavy cruiser *Chikuma* was attacked by four TBM Avengers, with *Manila Bay*'s Richard Deitchman hitting her with a Mk.13 torpedo which cut off her stern and disabled her port screw and rudder. *Chikuma*'s speed dropped to 18 knots then to half that, her steering inoperable.

At 11.05 hours, *Chikuma* was attacked by five TBMs from *Kitkun Bay* and two torpedoes struck her amidships. *Chikuma*'s end came when three more Avengers, led by Lieutenant Joseph Cady from *Natoma Bay*, hit the cruiser with yet more torpedoes. Here we see *Chikuma* just able to keep underway before she eventually sank – though her stern was cut off, her outboard propellers were still able to turn (USNHHC)

Above: Just three minutes after *Chikuma* had been hit on the 25th, *Chōkai* was also put out of action. Amazingly, it was probably the little 5-inch gun of *White Plains* which hit the heavy cruiser amidships. While the 20lb explosive payload of the shell could not pierce the hull of the powerful Japanese ship, it set off the eight deck-mounted Japanese Type 93 'Long Lance' torpedoes, which were especially volatile because they contained pure oxygen in addition to their 1,080lb warheads. The explosion resulted in such severe damage that it knocked out the rudder and engines, causing *Chōkai* to drop out of formation. A few minutes later, she was hit by a 500lb bomb which triggered fires that swept along the cruiser that left *Chōkai* dead in the water. She was duly abandoned, with the destroyer *Fujinami* taking off some of her crew before she was scuttled. (USNHHC)

Above: Shortly after the two Japanese cruisers had been disabled, something astonishing occurred. The powerful Centre Force of four battleships, six cruisers and twelve destroyers turned away from the action and began to retire. With two of his destroyers crippled and the aircraft from all three of Kinkaid's task units unrelenting in their attacks, Kurita simply gave up trying to destroy what he still considered might be the main Third Fleet's carrier force. This was a strange decision for a Japanese officer to make with their tradition of suicide rather than dishonour. In his battle report he justified his actions by claiming that he had received a message which indicated that there was a group of US carriers to the north of him and that he set off to try and engage them. 'Ziggy' Sprague later admitted that he could not believe his eyes when he saw the Japanese ships turn back.

Taffy 3 had suffered terrible losses in the battle, but this did not stop Sprague from despatching aircraft from *St. Lo* and *Kitkun Bay* to maintain pressure on the Japanese ships. Aircraft from carriers whose flight decks were unusable were landed on other carriers where they were re-armed, re-fuelled and sent back into action. But there was still one more twist in this remarkable tale.

At around 10.50 hours, the first 'organised' kamikaze attacks of the Pacific War were unleashed upon the American ships. All previous suicide efforts had been carried out either individually or impulsively.

THE BATTLE OFF SAMAR

The aircraft were from the Shikishima Special Attack Unit. Flying from the mainland, five A6M Zeros, led by Lieutenant Yukio Seki, set out to attack *Taffy 3*'s escort carriers.

This is the moment that one of the Zeros was shot down by a fighter from USS *Sangamon* during the kamikaze attacks off Leyte on 25 October 1944. The US aircraft was being flown by Lieutenant General Herman Weiss. (Historic Military Press)

Above: One of the kamikazes aimed for the bridge of *Kitkun Bay* but managed only to strike the port catwalk and cartwheel into the sea. Two others flew towards *Fanshaw Bay* but were shot down before they could reach the carrier. The final two attempted to slam into *White Plains*, with one of them veering off towards *St. Lo*.

The one that continued towards *White Plains* turned hard to try and avoid the carrier's gunfire, but shells poured into the aircraft which rolled over and exploded in the air, covering the flight deck with shrapnel as well as the gruesome remains of the pilot. Eleven men on the carrier were injured.[16] The scene in this photograph was taken as what was left of the Zero crashed into the sea. (US Navy)

BATTLE OF LEYTE GULF

Main image: Another suicide pilot, some accounts state that it was Lieutenant Yukio Seki himself, targeted *St. Lo*, managing to burst through the carrier's defensive fire. Orville Bethard was on *St. Lo* that fateful morning: 'Out of a rain squall came one lone airplane. And this plane came in and I saw that meatball on the side of it, so I knew it was Japanese … And this plane came in, probably twenty yards above the deck at the most.' The Zero was carrying a bomb, which it dropped, before it crashed into the flight deck of *St. Lo*. The bomb, Berthard explained, 'went through the wooden flight deck that we had and exploded in the hangar deck. And then he crashed his plane on the deck. *St. Lo* was rocked by fierce explosions as her aircraft munition ignited.' Here *St. Lo* is photographed being ripped apart by explosions. According to the after-action report following the first explosion, a second explosion blasted through the ship and was then, 'followed in a matter of seconds by a much more violent explosion, which rolled back a part of the flight deck … The next heavy explosion tore out more of the flight deck and also blew the elevator out of its shaft.'[17] *St. Lo* is seen here being ripped apart by explosions. (USNHHC)

THE BATTLE OFF SAMAR

Above: Some of the crew of USS *Kalinin Bay* watch as an explosion tears through USS *St. Lo* after she was hit be a kamikaze of Samar on 25 October. (National Museum of the US Navy)

Above: Attempting a kamikaze attack on USS *White Plains* off Samar, this Japanese A6M Zero crashed just off the carrier's port side. (National Museum of the US Navy)

BATTLE OF LEYTE GULF

Main image: Fires began to spread throughout *St. Lo*. Several men threw themselves overboard to escape the flames; others were blown into the sea. More explosions propelled large parts of the flight deck and even entire aircraft hundreds of feet into the air. At 11.00 hours, Captain McKenna ordered his crew to abandon ship. Further explosions tore out part of the hull and the carrier slumped to starboard. Large numbers of wounded men were lowered carefully into the water to join the others in the sea. (USNHHC)

THE BATTLE OFF SAMAR

Above: Another view of the stricken USS *St. Lo*. Most of the 889 men on board were rescued by the other ships of *Taffy 3*, seventy-five of whom were stretcher cases. Of the 889 men on board, 113 were killed or missing and approximately thirty others died of their wounds. The ship was abandoned only just in time. At 11.25 hours, under a dense cloud of smoke, *St. Lo* went down by the stern. Here we see *St. Lo* burning and being abandoned by her crew. *St. Lo* was the first major warship to be sunk by a kamikaze. (National Museum of the US Navy)

Opposite page: American survivors of the battle are rescued by a US Navy ship on 26 October 1944. Some 1,200 survivors of USS *Gambier Bay*, USS *Hoel*, USS *Johnston* and USS *Samuel B. Roberts* were rescued during the days following the action. (USNHHC)

Above: Altogether, 1,583 American sailors and airmen were killed or listed as missing and a further 913 were wounded in the battle. Materiel losses were two escort carriers, two destroyers and one escort destroyer sunk, with all the other ships of *Taffy 3* damaged. In addition, twenty-three aircraft were lost. This is a memorial service held on the flight deck of USS *Suwannee*, on 29 October 1944, to honour those crewmembers lost in the Battle of Leyte Gulf.

Kurita's Centre Force had, however, failed completely in its mission to disrupt the American landings

and had lost three heavy cruisers with a further three being damaged. Fifty-three aircraft were lost and later the destroyer *Nowaki*. Ozawa's Northern Force had successfully drawn the Third Fleet away from Leyte to present Kurita with an opportunity to cause serious harm to the Allied cause in the Pacific. Predictably, Kurita was severely criticised and was removed from his command in December. So strong was the sentiment against Kurita that to save him from assassination he was reassigned to the Imperial Japanese Naval Academy. (USNHHC)

Above: Vice Admiral Marc Mitscher was instrumental in the development of the Pacific Fleet's aircraft carrier force which by the time of the Battle of Leyte Gulf had become the most potent striking force in the Pacific theatre.

The large fleet carriers had from eighty-three to 101 planes each, in varying combinations of F6F Hellcat fighters, SB2C Helldiver bombers and TBF/TBM Avenger torpedo bombers. (USNHHC)

Chapter 6

BATTLE OFF CAPE ENGAÑO

25-26 October 1944

As soon as 'Bull' Halsey learned of the presence of Admiral Ozawa's Northern Force he decided to live up to his nickname and charge towards the enemy. Consequently, at 17.23 hours on the evening of 24 October, Vice Admiral Marc Mitscher, in command of the Fast Carrier Force Task Force 38, informed his task group commanders that he was going to move north-eastwards during the night to catch the Japanese carrier force the following morning.

Above: Mitscher's aircraft had not been able to keep constant contact with the Northern Force during the night, nevertheless, it was fully expected that by dawn the enemy would be within striking distance and the first waves were armed in the early hours ready to lift off as soon as it was light. Here 'Chockmen' are ready to pull chocks from the wheels of a Grumman F6F-2 Hellcat fighter, when given the order by the flight deck officer. (USNHHC)

Mitscher's Task Force 38 consisted of three carrier task groups – 38.2, 38.3 and 38.4. These, as we have learned, were told to concentrate at a point 150 miles north-east of San Bernardino Strait for the run north. Mitscher had a staggering fifteen fleet and light carriers under his control, which between them carried more than 1,000 aircraft. Supporting Task Force 38 was the rest of the Third Fleet comprising seven modern fast battleships, twenty-one cruisers and fifty-eight destroyers.

Meanwhile, Mitscher recommended that Task Force 34 should in fact be formed under Vice Admiral W.A. Lee (Commander, Battleships, Pacific Fleet), leaving Mitscher to direct the strikes against the Japanese carriers. His reasoning was that the battleships and cruisers, which moved much quicker than lumbering aircraft carriers, should intercept the enemy and hold them in position for Mitscher's aircraft to deliver the fatal blows. Halsey agreed. Task Force 34 was formed, leaving just a strong cordon of destroyers to protect the carriers.

The Japanese force was reported to comprise one fleet carrier, three light carriers, one converted carrier, one heavy and three light cruisers and six destroyers. On 7 December when the Japanese attacked Pearl Harbor, their carrier force was the most powerful in the Pacific, now it was weak and barely able to defend itself against the mighty American force that was bearing down on it. These carriers had just 116 aircraft, one-tenth the number of American machines that would soon be swooping down on them. Just one of those carriers that had attacked Pearl Harbor remained afloat, *Zuikaku*.

While the dramatic events were unfolding off Samar, Halsey's ships sighted Ozawa's Northern Force. They struck the Japanese in what is known as the Battle off Cape Engaño, the last of the engagements that together constitute the Battle of Leyte Gulf.

BATTLE OFF CAPE ENGAÑO

Main image: Dawn broke on the 25th to reveal a fine, clear day and scores of aircraft were despatched to track down the enemy carriers. The first Japanese ships to be sighted were two destroyers and then, at 07.30 hours, the main force was found, 135 miles to the north. Here a SB2C on USS *Lexington* is being loaded with fuel drop tanks before undertaking a search for the Northern Force. (USNHHC)

Above: Crewmen on the USS *San Jacinto* at work arming a TBM torpedo bomber of Torpedo Squadron 51 (VT-51) on 25 October 1944.

The photograph was probably taken before the squadron's planes attacked the Japanese carrier force during the Battle off Cape Engaño. The torpedo is a Mk.XIII fitted with a wooden stabilizer around its tail and drag ring around its nose. (US Navy)

Opposite page: The first wave of strike aircraft was already in the air fifty miles to the north and were, therefore, only eighty-five miles away when the Japanese ships were sighted. In half-an-hour they had the Japanese in their sights and at 08.40 hours they struck.

The *Essex*'s strike leader, Commander David McCampbell, who had so distinguished himself on the 24th, was made target coordinator and he assigned aircraft their targets as they arrived above the Northern Force. It was evident that the Japanese had been caught unawares as they had not launched all their aircraft, and the approaching US pilots only encountered around fifteen enemy fighters. These were swiftly despatched, which meant that McCampbell was able to stay unchallenged over the enemy throughout the entire engagement, directing the attack and reporting results.

Mitscher had made it clear that the enemy carriers were the prime target, but this was not always adhered to.

Having achieved his objective of luring the Third Fleet away from Letye Gulf, Ozawa tried to put as much distance as he could between his ships and those of the Third Fleet. The Japanese admiral was in no doubt, however, that he stood little chance of escaping: 'I expected complete destruction of my fleet, but if Kurita's mission was carried out, that was all I wished.' His Chief of Staff was equally committed: 'Surely we would be sunk; that was our mission.'[18]

In the ensuing chase the American carriers struggled to keep pace with those of the enemy. Though the Japanese were sailing northwards, Mitscher's carriers had to keep turning into the wind to land and launch their planes and the wind was coming from the east. 'Every available minute of time was devoted to gaining distance to the north,' wrote the commander of Task Group 38.4, Rear Admiral R.E. Davison in USS *Franklin*, 'yet the necessity for getting off the maximum air effort required frequent launchings and recoveries, and many planes with battle damage had to be taken aboard with varying degrees of urgency.'[19] An example of this can be seen in this photograph of a wounded Ensign A.A. Brauer being helped out of his F6F Hellcat aboard USS *Lexington*. (US Navy)

Above: The Helldiver bombers were the first to attack followed closely by the fighters, strafing the decks of the enemy ships to try and draw fire away from the dive bombers. The attacking aircraft were met with a heavy response from the main weapons of the cruisers and a barrage of anti-aircraft fire. Many aircraft were hit during the course of the day but, somewhat surprisingly, only ten were lost.

In the first attack, the light carrier *Chitose* was hit several times at least three of which were below the waterline. She staggered to a halt and sank at 09.37 hours. She rolled over to port and sank bow first, taking 903 men with her. Others of her crew, 501 in total, were rescued by the cruiser *Isuzu* and the destroyer *Shimotsuki*. *Chitose* is shown here earlier in 1944 after the conversion to a light carrier.

Opposite: *Chitose* was not the only casualty in the early exchanges. Another of the light carriers, *Zuihō*, seen here under attack from aircraft from USS *Essex*, managed to dodge all the bombs directed towards her except for one dropped by a dive-bomber operating from USS *Intrepid*. This, though, did not appear to slow the carrier down by any noticeable degree. (National Museum of the US Navy)

Below: Another of the Japanese aircraft carriers, in this case *Zuikaku*, the flagship of Admiral Ozawa's Northern Force, underway early in the action, while she was still capable of making good speed. Note the camouflage pattern painted on her flight deck and smoke coming from her stacks. (USNHHC)

BATTLE OFF CAPE ENGAÑO

BATTLE OF LEYTE GULF

Right: Zuihō under attack again, but still underway, this time by aircraft from USS Enterprise. Note the distinctive flight deck camouflage, the crewmen on deck, buckled flight deck amidships and mast deployed horizontally, with a Japanese naval ensign at its tip. (USNHHC)

Above: Pilots of Torpedo Squadron 51 discussing a mission following their return to USS San Jacinto after attacking the Japanese carrier force on 25 October 1944. One of VT-51's TBM torpedo planes is in the background. (NARA)

Overleaf: Zuikaku (left centre) and, probably, Zuihō (right) under attack. Both carriers are emitting heavy smoke and appear to be making good speed, indicating that this photograph was taken relatively early in the action. Note heavy concentration of anti-aircraft shell bursts in lower right and right, and a SB2C Helldiver diving in the lower left. (US Navy)

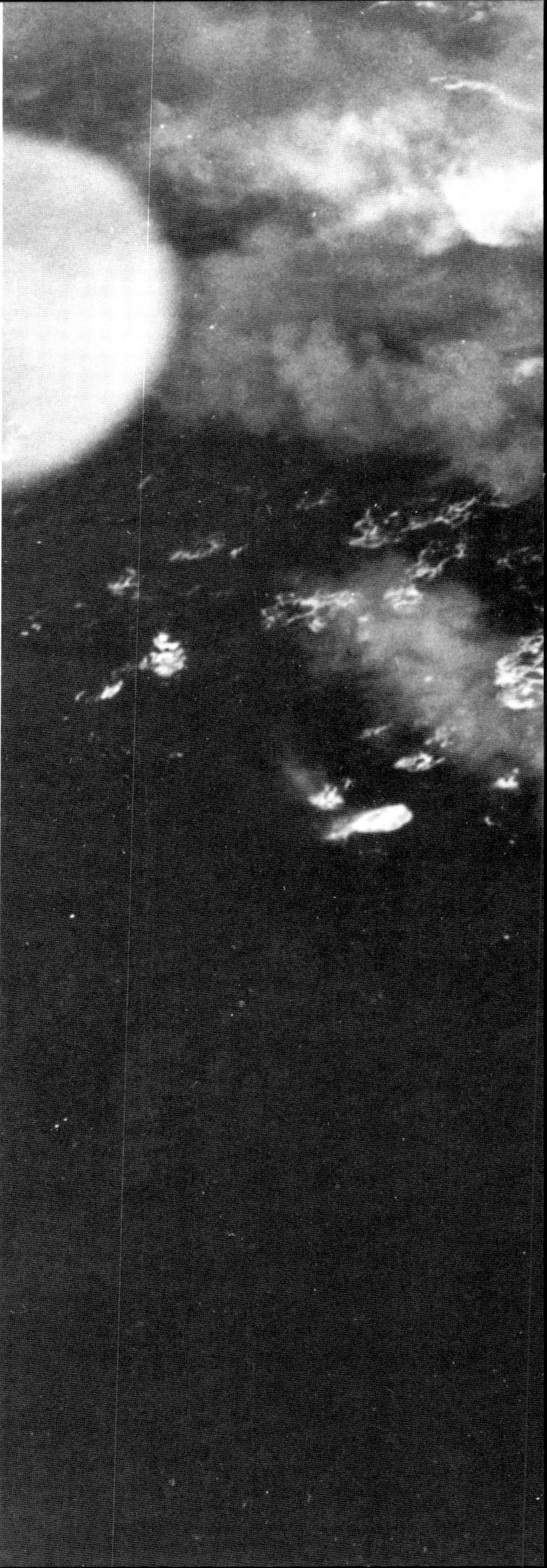

BATTLE OFF CAPE ENGAÑO

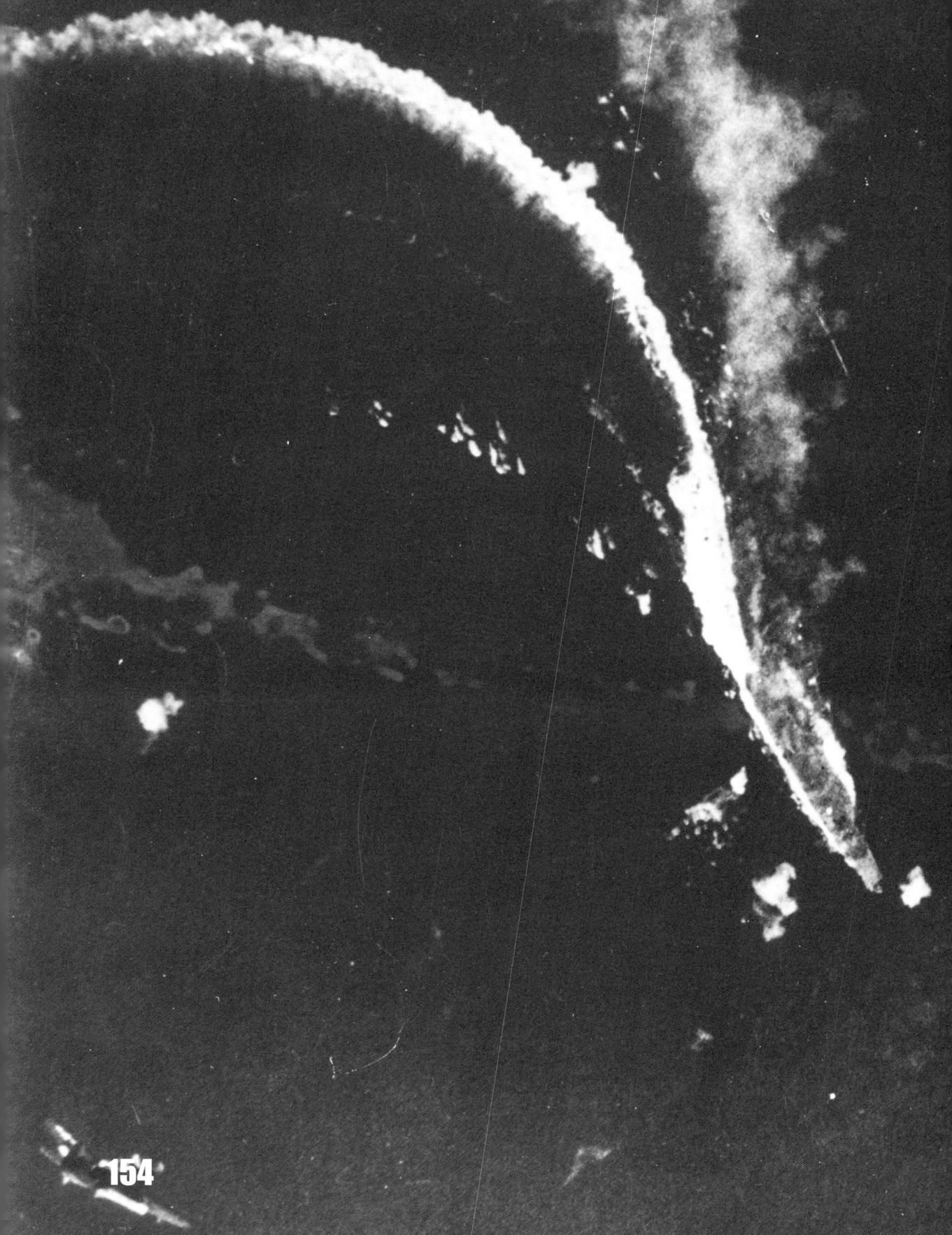

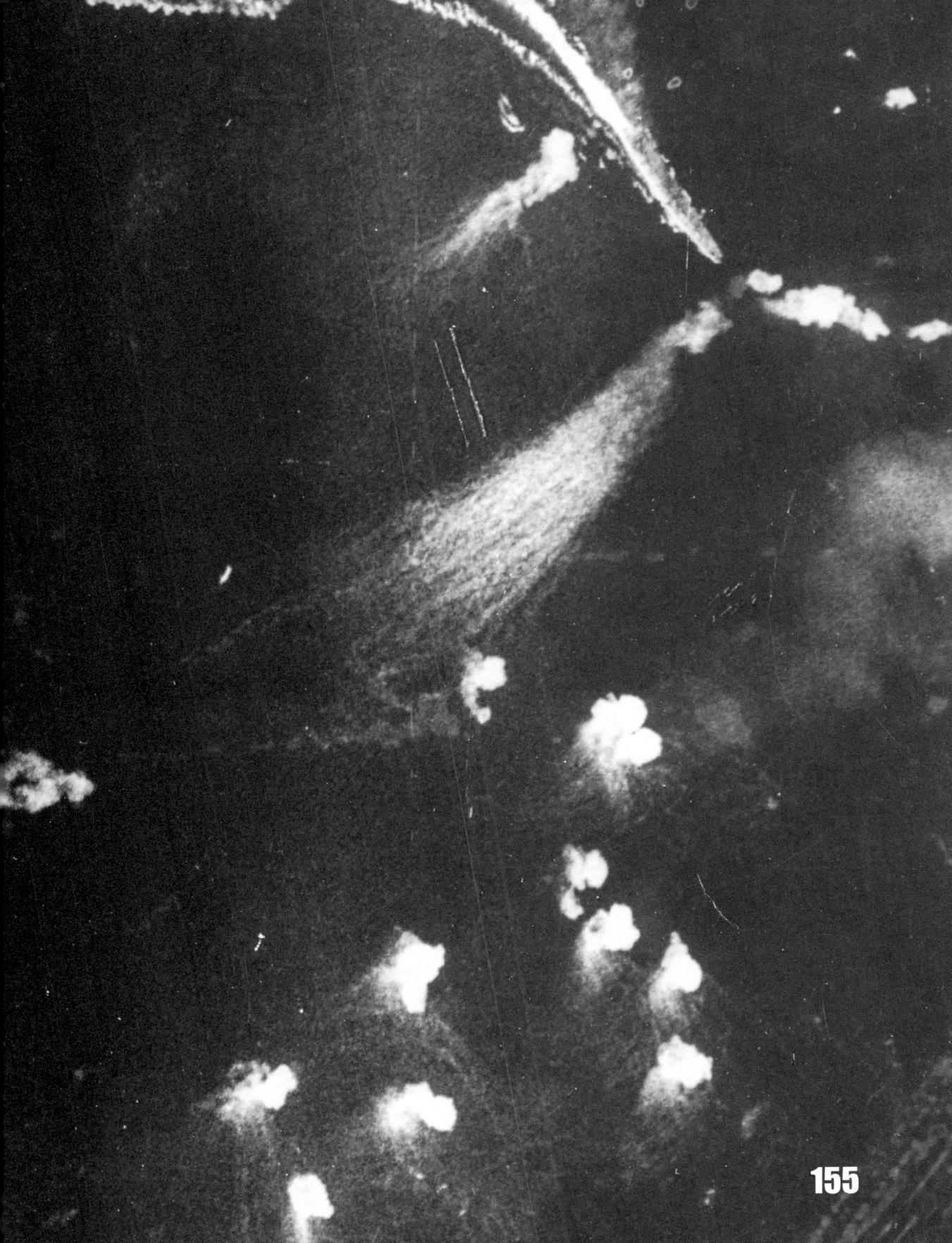

Above: The torpedo-bombers of *Intrepid* and *San Jacinto* launched torpedoes at *Zuikaku*, one of which struck her aft. She was seen to take on a slight list but, far more significantly, her communication system was knocked out and her steering control was damaged. *Zuikaku* was able to still make headway, though at a reduced speed of just 18 knots and her ability to manoeuvre was severely compromised, the crew having to steer her manually In this picture she is still moving northwards, but already the carrier is clearly in trouble. (USNHHC)

Below: In the first attack, the destroyer *Akizuki*, seen here, was 'mysteriously' sunk, probably by a torpedo, though no one claimed this ship as a victory. However, there were reports of a light cruiser suffering a 'violent explosion' due to a torpedo strike and this was most probably *Akizuki*. These large destroyers were sometimes mistaken as cruisers by the American pilots.

Above: An unknown cameraman caught this shot of the explosion aboard *Akizuki*. The original US Navy caption accompanying this photograph states that the damage appears to involve a large and intense fire in the vicinity of the ship's torpedo tube. It may, therefore, have been a secondary explosion which sealed the fate of the destroyer. (USNHHC)

Overleaf: There was no respite for the Northern Force, as the second strike-wave of US aircraft was already on its way. At around 10.00 hours, the Helldivers of *Lexington* and *Franklin* singled out *Chiyoda*. The light carrier was hit three times and she slowed to a halt. Ozawa ordered Admiral Matsuda Chiaki, with the converted carrier *Hyūga*, the light cruiser *Isuzu* and two destroyers to take *Chiyoda* in tow. This was a very strange decision. Ozawa was trying to get away with as many ships as he could, yet in detaching four ships to try and save one he was risking losing more of his command. Another light cruiser, *Tama*, was also hit in this second strike and though its speed was reduced to about 10 knots, she was still able to make headway.

This image shows Japanese ships manoeuvring to meet US air attacks during the early stages of the battle. It was taken from a TBM-1c from USS *San Jacinto*'s VT-51. Note the tight flak burst patterns across the centre of the picture. (USNHHC)

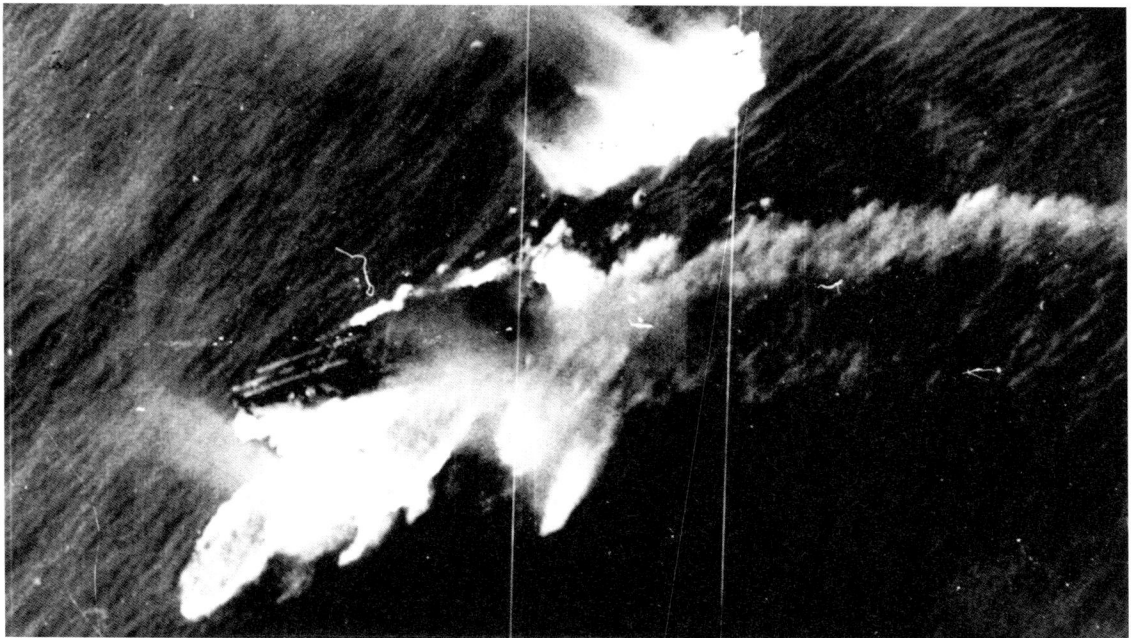

Above: Either *Chitose* or *Zuihō* under attack by Task Force 38 aircraft during the Battle off Cape Engaño, 25 October 1944. (USNHHC)

Opposite page top: There was then a lull in the air strikes, during which time Ozawa's staff tried to persuade him to transfer his flag from *Zuikaku*, whose communications had been knocked out, to the light cruiser *Ōyodo*. The admiral was reluctant to leave the carrier, apparently saying to his staff: 'What is the good? All my vessels are destined to be sunk. Out task is accomplished. I wish to die in *Zuikaku*.'[20] Nevertheless, he eventually agreed, and as seen in this photograph, he transferred to *Ōyodo* at around 11.00 hours.

That Ozawa had accomplished his task had also become apparent to Halsey when he received Kincaid's appeal for help. Kincaid repeated his calls to Halsey, but the Third Fleet's commander smelt blood and had no wish to turn back with the enemy so close. As he later admitted the chance to destroy the enemy fleet in a great surface encounter was 'the opportunity I had dreamt of since my days as a cadet.' But these appeals became more frantic, with Kincaid's fifth appeal reading: 'Enemy force attacked our CVEs [escort carriers composed of 4 bbs [battleships] 8 cruisers and other ships. Request Lee proceed top speed to cover Leyte. Request immediate strike bt fast carriers.'[21] The question posed by Kincaid and repeated by Admiral Nimitz at Pacific Fleet headquarters in Pearl Harbor: 'Where is rpt where is task force thirty four … the world wonders.' Lee's Task Force 34 was at that moment streaming at 25 knots towards the Northern Force and was too far away to be of any use to the Seventh Fleet.

Nevertheless, the only way the Third Fleet could possibly help Kincaid was by sending back some of its carriers, and, without waiting for orders, McCain turned round immediately with his five carriers and four heavy cruisers headed for Leyte Gulf as quickly as his ships could move. Even so, it would be hours before McCain would be close enough to launch his aircraft.

Halsey appeared to be in a state of paralysis, and when he eventually pulled himself together,

following further and even more desperate sounding appeals from Kincaid, he made yet another mistake. He ordered Lee to break off his pursuit of the Northern Force and return to help Kincaid. Force 34 was only forty-five miles from Ozawa's force and closing rapidly, but Halsey threw away his chance of completely destroying the Northern Force. Halsey informed Kincaid that he was on his way back but that he could not be expected until 08.00 hours the following morning – when, of course, it would be far too late. It should be born in mind, that the 16-inch guns of Halsey's battleships had a range of just over twenty miles, which meant that when he turned back, his ships were only twenty-five miles from being able to engage the Japanese.

Halsey broke up the Third Fleet causing considerable delay while units were brought together and refuelled while he reorganised his command. He sent Rear Admiral Gerald Bogan's Task Force 38.2, which included the carriers *Intrepid*, *Cabot* and *Independence*, south to follow McCain, at the same time detaching the heavy cruisers *Wichita* and *New Orleans* and the light cruisers *Santa Fe* and *Mobile* with ten destroyers to provide protection for Brogan's carriers.

Task Force 34 was then broken up, Halsey forming a new grouping, Task Force 34.5 with the two fast battleships *Iowa* and his flagship *New Jersey* and raced off to help Kincaid, leaving Brogan far in its wake. The Third Fleet was now in four parts spread across the Philippine Sea. Halsey was later to concede that his decision to turn back was his 'gravest error', yet it merely compounded his earlier mistakes. His actions meant that the forces sent southwards were far too late to be of any value in the Battle off Samar and the force left in the north was not powerful enough to complete the destruction of Ozawa's force. Halsey, with more firepower at his disposal than the entire Japanese Imperial Navy contrived to waste his main strength steaming backwards and forwards without it engaging the enemy.

Everything then depended on Mitscher's remining aircraft. Ozawa still had fifteen ships afloat, it was to be seen how many of these the US pilots could sink before nightfall. (USNHHC)

BATTLE OFF CAPE ENGAÑO

Opposite page: The third raid was the largest of the day, totalling more than 200 aircraft. They reached the Japanese ships at 13.10 hours. *Zuikaku* and *Zuihō* were the targets of aircraft from *Essex*, *Lexington* and *Langley*. Here a Matsu-class destroyer is firing at planes as a carrier in the background is bombed. (US Navy)

Right: *Zuihō*, seen here during the battle, was hit several times and fires were started though her speed remained undiminished. (USNHHC)

Below: It was quite a different story for *Zuikaku*. The last great Japanese carrier was hit by both torpedoes and bombs, drifting to a dead stop. *Zuikaku* and *Zuihō* under attack viewed from an aircraft from *Franklin*. *Zuikaku* is on fire to the right of the photograph. (USNHHC)

163

BATTLE OF LEYTE GULF

Opposite page top: *Zuikaku* under attack by aircraft of the USS Enterprise's Air Group Twenty, 25 October 1944. (National Museum of the US Navy)

Opposite page bottom: *Zuikaku* rapidly took on water and began to list to port. Here, crew members are throwing ammunition overboard to prevent a possible explosion. (USNHHC)

Below: At 13.27 hours, with *Zuikaku* now at an angle of 21 degrees, all hands were called on deck. The ship's ensign was lowered, and at 13.58 hours the order to abandon ship was given. In this dramatic photograph, members of *Zuikaku*'s crew can be seen saluting the Japanese Naval Ensign as it is lowered on the carrier for the last time.

At 14.14 hours, *Zuikaku* rolled over and sank stern-first, taking Rear Admiral Kaizuka Takeo and 842 of the ship's crew with her. (USNHHC)

BATTLE OF LEYTE GULF

Above: The fourth raid of the day was delivered thirty minutes later by around forty aircraft, which directed their attack upon *Zuihō* and the battleship *Ise*, the latter shown here firing her main guns during the Battle off Cape Engaño. The photograph was taken by an aircraft operating from the aircraft carrier USS *Essex*. (USNHHC)

Opposite page: A battleship of the Japanese Ise-class under attack on 25 October 1944. According to one source this is *Ise* itself. (NARA)

Below: As a result of excellent seamanship and good gunnery, *Ise* successfully avoided all the torpedoes fired at her and was only hit by one bomb – at which point this picture was taken. Striking near the battleship's port catapult, this bomb killed five crewmen and wounded seventy-one others. The near-misses did also cause some damage, such as to the hull plating near the waterline. (National Museum of the US Navy)

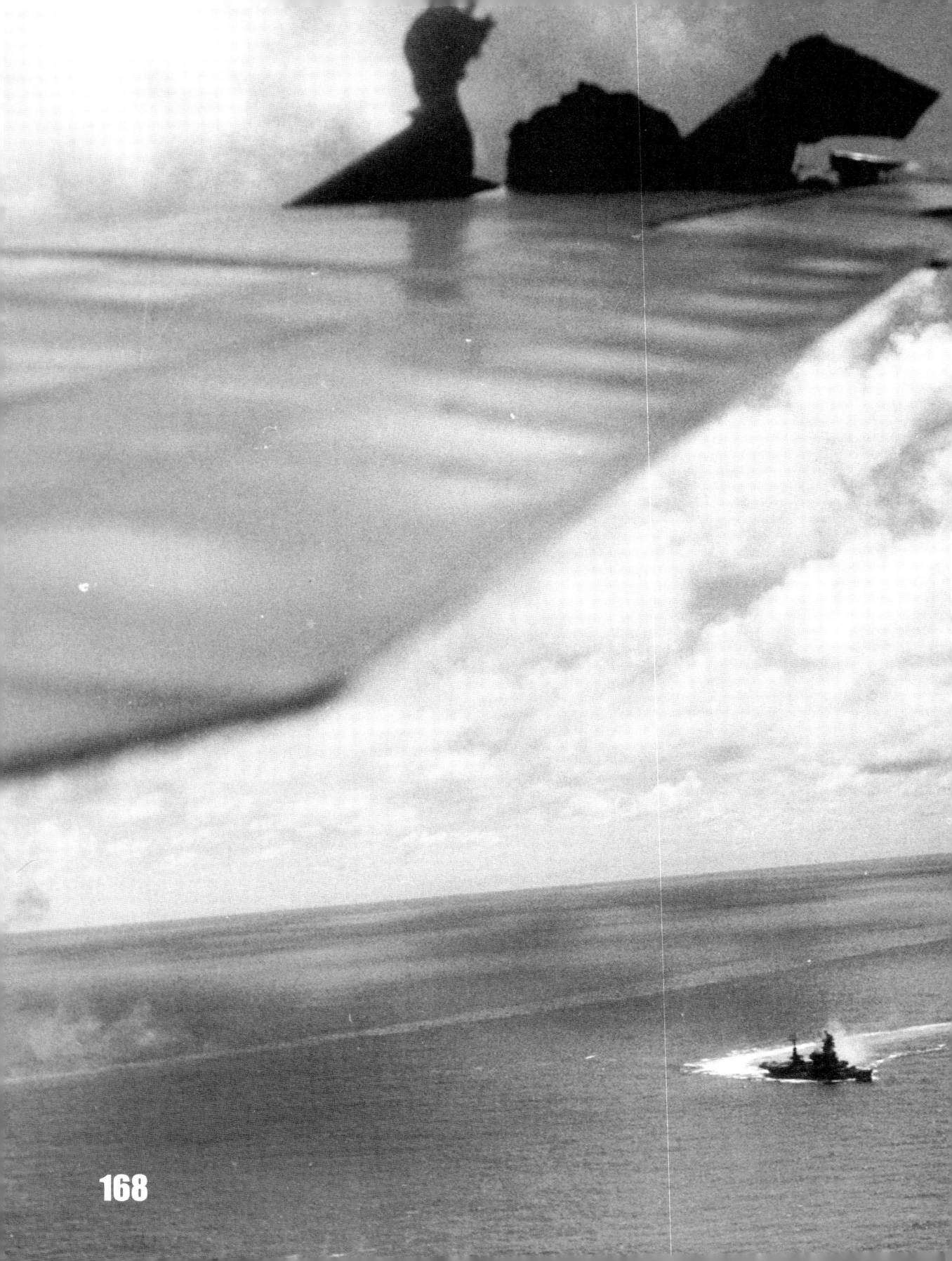

BATTLE OFF CAPE ENGAÑO

Above: Almost thirty of the attacking aircraft concentrated on *Zuihō* and she was hit with at least two bombs and two torpedoes. Here, she is under sustained attack. (USNHHC)

Left: Another photograph of *Ise* in action alongside an Akizuki-class destroyer, this one taken by a TBM from USS *San Jacinto*. Note the damaged wingtip on the aircraft. (USNHHC)

Below: After the repeated attacks, *Zuihō* began to list to port and despite all hands manning the pumps, at 15.10 hours the order was given to abandon ship. At 15.26 hours, *Zuihō* began to slide under the waves, with 215 men losing their lives. (USNHHC)

BATTLE OF LEYTE GULF

Above: The fifth attack of the day upon the Northern Force was delivered at around 17.00 hours. Approximately 100 planes from *Enterprise*, *Essex*, *Langley*, *Franklin* and *Lexington* swooped in to finish off the rest of Ozawa's beleaguered force. This time, despite numerous claims of hitting *Ise* and *Hyūga*, no real damage was done to these two warships. Astonishingly, *Ise* reported thirty-four near misses. It is either *Ise* or *Hyūga* which is shown here firing on attacking US naval aircraft during the battle. Note the gunfire by the ship's main battery. (NARA)

Right: The final aerial attack was undertaken by a force of thirty-six aircraft from *San Jacinto*, *Enterprise* and *Franklin*. It took place an hour later but, with night drawing in, they failed to hit any of the Japanese ships. The Northern Force was still not out of danger, as a line of submarines waited for Ozawa's unsuspecting captains, while Mitscher had detached a force of cruisers and destroyers under Rear Admiral Lawrence DuBose to maintain the pursuit. DuBose's flagship was the light cruiser *Santa Fe* seen here. (USNHHC)

BATTLE OF LEYTE GULF

Above: DuBose came upon *Chiyoda* which had been abandoned to its fate by *Isuzu* and the two destroyers detached to try and save her. At 16.25 hours *Wichita* and *New Orleans* opened fire on *Chiyoda* with their 8-inch guns. *Chiyoda* tried to fight back with her 127mm anti-aircraft guns, but it really was no contest and the two U.S. cruisers hammered shell after shell into the Japanese carrier until she was a burning, smoking wreck. DuBose then sent his destroyers in to finish off *Chiyoda* with their torpedoes but she capsized and sank at 16.50 hours before the destroyers could get in on the act. *Chiyoda* is seen here, from USS *Wichita*, on fire after being hit by the American cruisers which opened fire at a range of 20,000 yards. Captain Jō Eiichirō and the entire crew of 1,470 officers and men went down with the ship. (NARA)

Right: The next Japanese ships to be engaged by DuBose's force were three destroyers which had been trying to pick up survivors from *Zuikaku* and *Zuihō*, including the large *Hatsuzuki* which put up a still fight until after dark, even managing to fire torpedoes at DuBose's flagship. Dubose was able to return the compliment, sending in destroyers under cover of the gunfire from the cruisers which sent at least two torpedoes into the side of the Japanese ship. The torpedo strikes slowed *Hatsuzuki* down to ten knots and the US cruisers moved in for the kill. Here shells from the light carrier USS *Mobile* strike the Japanese destroyer. (USNHHC)

173

BATTLE OF LEYTE GULF

Left: The cruisers closed up to 6,000 yards from the crippled destroyer, pouring shells into what had become a mangled, burning wreck. DuBose instructed the captain of the destroyer *Porterfield* to 'put a fish in him' and finish *Hatsuzuki* off, but, as before, she sank before the destroyer could do its work. The brave efforts of *Hatsuzuki* enabled the other two Japanese destroyers to slip away. Lawrence T. DuBose, seen here, went on to reach the rank of Vice Admiral. (USNHHC)

Below: Ozawa did rush back to try and save *Hatsuzuki*, but the destroyer had long since sunk beneath the Pacific and he led his remaining ships back towards home. In the dark, the US submarines managed to sink only one enemy ship, this was the light cruiser *Tama*, which went down amid a flurry of torpedoes at 23.05 hours fired from USS *Pintado* and USS *Jallao*. The latter is shown here in 1944. This was the last of Ozawa's ships to go down. Ozawa had played his part in the operation perfectly and escaped with ten ships still afloat. (US Navy)

Chapter 7

CONSEQUENCES AND CONTROVERSIES

The fighting was not quite over. Halsey, it may be recalled, was trying to make amends for his mistakes by racing as rapidly as he could with his two fastest battleships, *Iowa* and *New Jersey*, three light cruisers and eight destroyers to cut off Kurita's escape through the San Bernardino Strait.

Halsey, though, was too late to intercept the remnants of the Centre Force, except for the destroyer *Nowake* which had spent time picking up survivors from the heavy cruiser *Chikuma*. *Nowake* was engaged by the destroyers USS *Millar* and USS *Owen* with torpedoes and gunfire. It was most probably torpedoes from the latter which finished off *Nowake*.

Above: In this photograph, a number of the key characters in the battle are pictured together. From left to right are Clifton Spruance, Marc Mitscher, Chester Nimitz and Vice Admiral Willis A. Lee, Jr., the man who was designated to form the phantom Task Force 34. (USNHHC)

Reconnaissance aircraft of Night Air Group 41, VF(N)-41 from one of Admiral Bogan's carriers, USS *Independence*, spotted Kurita's main force and tracked it through the night until contact was lost due to a thunderstorm. The Japanese ships were sighted once more at 08.00 hours on the 26th, and strike groups from both McCain's and Bogan's carriers attacked thirty minutes later. Though claims were made by the American flyers, no serious damage was inflicted on the enemy. Air strikes continued throughout the day and while some of Kurita's ships may have been hit, none were sunk.

There was, though, one scalp the Americans could claim. As Admiral Shima's Second Striking Force returned to home waters, it was attacked by USAAF B-24 bombers. The already badly damaged *Abukuma* was hit, in what was a rare case of high-altitude heavy bombers actually hitting a ship, resulting in her torpedo bank detonating. The light cruiser sank with the loss of 250 of her crew.

Over the next days, US carrier aircraft picked off several more Japanese light cruisers (*Noshiro* and *Kinu*) and destroyers, but the Battle of Leyte Gulf was effectively over. It was by some, though not all, measured as the largest naval engagement of all time. It involved 200,000 men and spanned

Above: There were approximately 3,000 Allied casualties during the various engagements and here bodies are being transferred before being buried at sea. (USNHHC)

more than 100,000 square miles. It included some of the largest and most powerful warships ever built. The greatest naval battle of the First World War, Jutland, involved more ships, 254 compared with 244 at Leyte, but the total tonnage at the latter was 2,014,890 tons versus 1,616,836 in 1916.

Total Japanese losses amounted to twenty-six ships, of which three were battleships. In addition, there was one fleet and three light carriers, six heavy and four light cruisers, and nine destroyers. Total weight of shipping lost was 305,710 tons. It was the greatest loss the Japanese Navy had ever suffered.

The Japanese plan came close to working, but the result was a decisive US Navy victory that effectively ended any future serious opposition from the Imperial Japanese Navy, at least from surface ships. That being the case, Halsey's poor performance is perhaps only relevant in that it cost the lives of 1,583 U.S. sailors of *Taffy 3*.

Certainly, this loss justifiably angered Kincaid who wrote the following in his official report: 'At 15.12 on 24th October, Commander Third Fleet issued a despatch, which was intercepted by

Above: A funeral service underway on USS *Kalanin Bay* for some of those killed during the Battle of Leyte Gulf. (USNHHC)

Commander Seventh Fleet, to all Third Fleet subordinate commands, stating that a force of battleships, cruisers, and destroyers was being formed as Task Force 34, presumably to engage the Japanese Central Force. Commander Task Force 38 reported at 18.52 that planes had sighted another Japanese force, hereafter referred to as the Northern Force …

'At 20.24 Commander Third Fleet advised Commander Seventh Fleet that the enemy Centre Force … was moving on a course of 120°, speed 12kn [knots], in Sibuyan Sea towards the northwest tip of Masbate Island (in the direction of San Bernardino Strait). He further stated that he was "proceeding north with three groups to attack the enemy carrier force (Northern Force) at dawn. As the fast battleships had been removed from the carrier groups and organised as Task Force 34, it was assumed that Task Force 34 was still guarding San Bernardino Strait."[22]

This was the start of the dispute between the two fleet commanders.

Halsey was not officially sanctioned for his performance and he later sought to vindicate his actions, writing the following: 'That they (the Japanese Centre Force) might attempt to transit San Bernardino Strait, despite their fearful mauling, was a possibility I had to recognize. Accordingly, at 15.12 I sent a preparatory dispatch to all Task Force Commanders in the Third Fleet and all Task Group Commanders in Task Group 38, designating four of their fast battleships, with supporting units, and stating that these ships will be formed as Task Force 34 under Vice Admiral Lee, Commander Battle Line, with the mission of engaging decisively at long ranges.

'This dispatch, which played a critical part in next day's battle, I intended merely as a warning to the ships concerned that, if a surface engagement offered, I would detach them from Task Force 38, form them into Task Force 34, and send them ahead as a battle line. It was definitely not an executive dispatch, but a battle plan, and was so marked. To make certain that none of my subordinate commanders misconstrued it, I told them later by voice radio: "IF THE ENEMY SORTIES, TASK FORCE 34 WILL BE FORMED WHEN DIRECTED BY ME."'

The following year, Halsey bumped into Clifton Sprague at Ulithi for the first time since the battle. 'I didn't know if you would speak to me or not,' said Halsey. Sprague replied that he bore Halsey no malice. To this Halsey answered, to his credit, that 'I want you to know I think you wrote the most glorious page in American naval history that day.' Halsey continued to praise 'Ziggy' so effusively, wrote Halsey's biographer, that Sprague called it 'embarrassing'. But it was Halsey's way of saying that he accepted that he had made an error in leaving the Seventh Fleet unprotected.[23]

Though the controversy still rages, and Halsey's actions continue to be debated in public and in print, if the two admirals can end their differences there, then we can end this story at that point also.

Opposite page top: A Japanese warship under air attack to the south of Masbate, Philippines, on 26 October 1944. This is possibly a Kuma-class cruiser, either *Kinu* or *Abukuma*, both of which were sunk on this day, or the destroyer *Uranami*. This is a still from gun camera footage from an aircraft operating from USS *Sangamon*. (USNHHC)

Opposite page bottom: The crews of the 40mm guns of USS *Sangamon* remain on alert on 26 October 1944, having been attacked a few minutes earlier. (USNHHC)

Overleaf: A Japanese destroyer under air attack off southern Mindoro on 26 October 1944, during the pursuit of the Japanese fleet after the main battles. Photographed by an aircraft from USS *Cowpens*. (USNHHC)

CONSEQUENCES AND CONTROVERSIES

Above: Sailors assigned to the aircraft carrier USS *Nimitz* conduct a 21-gun salute during a Battle of Leyte Gulf commemoration ceremony in the Surigao Strait, July 2017. Nimitz was on deployment in the US 7th Fleet area of operations at the time. (US Navy)

Opposite page: A memorial to the Battle of Leyte Gulf stands by the seafront at San Diego. While officially called the Memorial to Admiral Sprague and Task Unit 77.4.3, it is generally known as the Taffy 3 Memorial. The memorial consists of thirteen panels, one for each ship of *Taffy 3*, in the centre of which is a bust of 'Ziggy' Sprague. Below the bust is the Presidential Unit Citation, which reads in part:

'Silhouetted against the dawn as the Central Japanese Force steamed through San Bernardino Strait towards Leyte Gulf, Task Unit 77.4.3 was suddenly taken under attack by hostile cruisers on its port

CONSEQUENCES AND CONTROVERSIES

hand, destroyers on the starboard and battleships from the rear. Quickly laying down a heavy smoke screen, the gallant ships of the Task Unit waged battle fiercely against the superior speed and fire power of the advancing enemy, swiftly launching and rearming aircraft and violently zigzagging in protection of vessels stricken by hostile armor-piercing shells, anti-personnel projectiles and suicide bombers. With one carrier of the group sunk, others badly damaged and squadron aircraft courageously coordinating in the attacks by making dry runs over the enemy Fleet as the Japanese relentlessly closed in for the kill, two of the Unit's valiant destroyers and one destroyer escort charged the battleships point-blank and, expending their last torpedoes in desperate defense of the entire group, went down under the enemy's heavy shells as a climax to two and one half hours of sustained and furious combat.'

REFERENCES AND NOTES

1. General Staff, *Reports of General MacArthur: The Campaigns of MacArthur in the Pacific*, Vol. I (Washington D.C., 1966), p.196.
2. Anon, *United States Strategic Bombing Survey (Pacific), Naval Analysis Division, Interrogations of Japanese Officials*, Vol. II, p.317.
3. General Staff, *Reports of General MacArthur: The Campaigns of MacArthur in the Pacific*, Vol. I (Washington D.C., 1966), p.198.
4. The National Archives (TNA), ADM 234/365 *The Battle for Leyte Gulf*, p.27.
5. Thomas J. Cutler, *The Battle of Leyte Gulf, 23-26 October 1944* (HarperCollins, 1994, New York), p.131.
6. Akira Yoshimura, *Battleship Musashi: The Making And Sinking Of The World's Biggest Battleship* (Kodansha International, Tokyo, 1999), p.175.
7. TNA ADM 234/365.
8. Roland Smoot, *The Reminiscences of Vice Admiral Roland N. Smoot* (Annapolis, U.S. Naval Institute Press, 1972), p.139.
9. See: www.combinedfleet.com.
10. *Eyewitness to the Battle off Samar and the Loss of the USS St. Lo*, nationalww2museum.org.
11. John Toland, *Rising Sun, The Decline and Fall of the Japanese Empire 1936-1945* (Pen & Sword, Barnsley, 2011), p.565.
12. Jean Hood, *Carrier: A Century of First-Hand Accounts of Naval Operations in War and Peace* (Conway, London, 2010), p.249.
13. Cutler, op.cit, pp.245-6.
14. 'The First Kamikaze' *Navy Medicine* 85, no. 5 (Sep.-Oct. 1994), pp. 6-11. For his heroic work on *Suwannee*, Lieutenant Burwell received the Silver Star.
15. Quoted from www.ussgambierbay.org.
16. Adrian Stewart, *The Battle of Leyte Gulf* (Robert Hale, London, 1979), p.199.
17. Quoted from the National World War II Museum's Digital Collection.
18. Stewart, op. cit, p.122.
19. TNA, ADM 234/365.
20. Stewart, op. cit, p.130.
21. John Wukovits, *Admiral "Bull" Halsey, The Life and Wars of the Navy's Most Controversial Commander* (Palgrave Macmillan, New York, 2010), p.197.
22. TNA, ADM 234/365.
23. Wukovits, op. cit, p.209.